CALENDARS OF THE WORLD

Full of amazing facts and a wealth of detail, *Calendars of the World* takes the reader on a trip through time and around the world as it charts the growth and development of the world's various timekeeping systems. Some calendars thrive and others fail, but all are interestingly detailed by an author with a love for her subject.

ABOUT THE AUTHOR: Margo Westrheim, a teacher for over thirty-five years, has been researching and writing about timekeeping systems for the past decade. Raised in the USA, but now a Canadian citizen, her other interests include multicultural education and inter-faith understanding. She is married with two daughters, five grandchildren and a computer-literate cat named Samson.

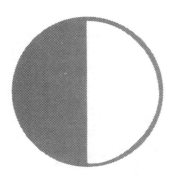

CALENDARS OF THE WORLD

A LOOK AT CALENDARS
& THE WAYS WE CELEBRATE

Margo Westrheim

ONEWORLD

OXFORD

*T*his book is lovingly dedicated to Alice Wood Kerr, the friend who first aroused my interest in the importance of calendars and their relationship to culture and religion.

ACKNOWLEDGEMENTS

The author is grateful to the following for permission to reproduce illustrations: *Illustration 2* Based on a drawing by Chandra Madhosingh, Vancouver, BC. *Illustrations 4 & 5* From *Book of the Gods and Rites and the Ancient Calendar*, by Fray Diego Duran. The Bodleian Library, University of Oxford (948.d.42). Copyright © 1971, University of Oklahoma Press. *Illustration 6* Adapted from *Living the Sky* by Ray A. Williamson, Houghton Mifflin Company, New York, N.Y. *Illustration 7* Drawing by Snowden Hodges from *Living the Sky* by Ray A. Williamson, Houghton Mifflin Company, New York, N.Y. Copyright © 1984 Snowden Hodges. *Illustration 11* From *The Story of Our Calendar* by Ruth Brindze, The Vanguard Press, New York, N.Y. *Illustration 12* From the Edward Clark Streeter Collection of Weights and Measures, Yale University, New Haven, Conn. *Illustration 13* Adapted from *The Bahá'ís*, a publication of the Bahá'í International Community. *Illustrations 14–18* By kind permission of UNICEF.

Calendars of the World

Oneworld Publications
Sales and Editorial
185 Banbury Road
Oxford OX2 7AR, England

Oneworld Publications
42 Broadway
Rockport
MA 01966, U.S.A.

© Margo Westrheim, 1993
All rights reserved
Copyright under Berne Convention

A CIP record for this book is available from the British Library

ISBN 1-85168-051-9

Printed & bound by
Werner Söderström Osakeyhtiö,
Finland

CONTENTS

ILLUSTRATIONS

TABLES

INTRODUCTION

Every day of our lives we are influenced by calendars – those very convenient ways of measuring time. Calendars have helped generations of people know when to worship, work, play, go to school, celebrate special occasions, make and keep appointments. Most of us feel quite comfortable living with the regular rhythm of the Gregorian calendar with its seven-day week, content with its accuracy in measuring out our time.

Our ancient ancestors were not so lucky, struggling for many generations to develop good timekeeping systems. Although they lacked computers and modern technology to help them solve the challenge of measuring time, they did have the intelligence and skills to meet the challenge, coupled with finely tuned powers of observation. This book takes a look at some of the problems our ancestors encountered and the fascinating and creative ways they chose to measure time and organize it into convenient units.

For lo, the winter is past …
The flowers appear on the earth …
The fig tree putteth forth her green figs …
– Song of Solomon

	JANUARY	FEBRUARY	MARCH
MONDAY	4 11 18 25	1 8 15 22	1 8 15 22 29
TUESDAY	5 12 19 26	2 9 16 23	2 9 16 23 30
WEDNESDAY	6 13 20 27	3 10 17 24	3 10 17 24 31
THURSDAY	7 14 21 28	4 11 18 25	4 11 18 25
FRIDAY	1 8 15 22 29	5 12 19 26	5 12 19 26
SATURDAY	2 9 16 23 30	6 13 20 27	6 13 20 27
SUNDAY	3 10 17 24 31	7 14 21 28	7 14 21 28

	APRIL	MAY	JUNE
MONDAY	5 12 19 26	3 10 17 24 31	7 14 21 28
TUESDAY	6 13 20 27	4 11 18 25	1 8 15 22 29
WEDNESDAY	7 14 21 28	5 12 19 26	2 9 16 23 30
THURSDAY	1 8 15 22 29	6 13 20 27	3 10 17 24
FRIDAY	2 9 16 23 30	7 14 21 28	4 11 18 25
SATURDAY	3 10 17 24	1 8 15 22 29	5 12 19 26
SUNDAY	4 11 18 25	2 9 16 23 30	6 13 20 27

	JULY	AUGUST	SEPTEMBER
MONDAY	5 12 19 26	2 9 16 23 30	6 13 20 27
TUESDAY	6 13 20 27	3 10 17 24 31	7 14 21 28
WEDNESDAY	7 14 21 28	4 11 18 25	1 8 15 22 29
THURSDAY	1 8 15 22 29	5 12 19 26	2 9 16 23 30
FRIDAY	2 9 16 23 30	6 13 20 27	3 10 17 24
SATURDAY	3 10 17 24 31	7 14 21 28	4 11 18 25
SUNDAY	4 11 18 25	1 8 15 22 29	5 12 19 26

	OCTOBER	NOVEMBER	DECEMBER
MONDAY	4 11 18 25	1 8 15 22 29	6 13 20 27
TUESDAY	5 12 19 26	2 9 16 23 30	7 14 21 28
WEDNESDAY	6 13 20 27	3 10 17 24	1 8 15 22 29
THURSDAY	7 14 21 28	4 11 18 25	2 9 16 23 30
FRIDAY	1 8 15 22 29	5 12 19 26	3 10 17 24 31
SATURDAY	2 9 16 23 30	6 13 20 27	4 11 18 25
SUNDAY	3 10 17 24 31	7 14 21 28	5 12 19 26

ILLUSTRATION 1. A modern Gregorian year calendar as widely used today.

Different cultures and different living conditions resulted in a host of varied and interesting solutions to the riddle of measuring time around the world and throughout history. But when we study timekeeping systems it soon emerges that, over time, our ancestors around the world developed many common ways to keep track of time and also chose similar ways to celebrate their sacred and secular events.

Imagine the joy the first signs of spring brought to peoples in ancient times. If you lived in a country with bitterly cold winters, you would have felt like celebrating when the warmth of spring caused green buds to appear on trees and shrubs. If you lived in a country with a long, hot, dry season, you would have felt like celebrating when the rains of the wet season caused grasses to sprout. This seasonal renewal of life has always brought elation, courage and hope to the inhabitants of earth.

For our ancestors, there were many important events in their lives that were worth celebrating or commemorating, many of them seemingly simple, but vital for their survival. These might include the time for planting; the time for harvesting; the coming of age of young people; the marriage of a chieftain; or the death of a ruler or a holy person. For most of these occasions seasonal changes or phases of the moon were quite good enough for telling the time and deciding when to celebrate.

But it became important to our forebears to set aside specific times for what they saw as necessary religious and sacred acts:

To give praise and thanksgiving to their god;
To pray, fast, worship and sacrifice;
To purify themselves for sacred service ;
To beg their god's forgiveness and ask for mercy;
To hold festivals in remembrance of the prophets
  and messengers of their god.

How could they know when the correct time was to offer thanksgiving, to sacrifice, to fast, to worship, to pray? The seasonal clock (see

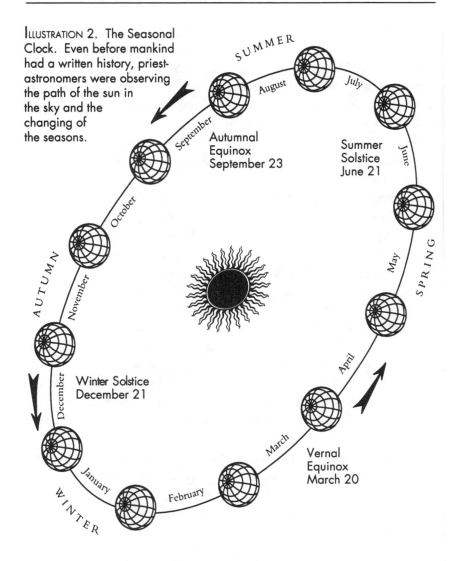

ILLUSTRATION 2. The Seasonal Clock. Even before mankind had a written history, priest-astronomers were observing the path of the sun in the sky and the changing of the seasons.

SUMMER

August

July

September

Autumnal Equinox September 23

Summer Solstice June 21

June

October

AUTUMN

SPRING

May

November

April

December

Winter Solstice December 21

March

January

Vernal Equinox March 20

February

WINTER

Illustration 2) and the star clock in the sky no longer answered all their needs.

As it became important to people to honor sacred occasions and events, they needed to know not only in which season but also on which day and in which month the occasion occurred. Ancient peoples became more and more anxious to be able to determine the correct time to celebrate such significant events as the birthday of the founder of their religion, the date of his enlightenment or revelation, the dates of his victories and triumphs, and the dates of his tragedies and death.

Many wise people knew that the sun, moon and stars were their guides in keeping track of time. They studied, observed and charted the movements of the sun and stars, and the phases of the moon. They became very skillful in their calculations and began to record their patient observations carefully in order to develop methods for measuring and organizing time. What they eventually designed was what we now call a calendar. And while designing a workable calendar, these wise people also discovered and developed the sciences of astronomy and mathematics, to the lasting benefit of mankind.

This book chronicles their achievements, and draws attention to the many threads of unity in the worldwide attempts of humankind to measure the passage of time and decide when to celebrate.

SOME PROBLEMS IN MEASURING TIME

He appointed the
moon for
seasons;
The sun knoweth
his going down.
– Psalm 104:19

In ancient times there were certain elders in the tribes who were responsible for memorizing and safeguarding the collective wisdom of their people and passing it on to the next generation. A select few of the elders held and guarded the secrets of the tribe's religious ceremonies and rituals, or the knowledge learned from watching the course of the sun, the phases of the moon and the movements of the stars. To describe these select few men and women in modern terms, it could be said that they had the power of a priest and the skills of an astronomer.

When it came to learning how to measure time and to develop timekeeping systems and calendars, the priest-astronomers of ancient times had many challenges to meet and problems to solve. One of those problems was how to divide time into convenient units and how long those units should be. The most popular, and the easiest to measure, unit of time was the period we know as the day. The first popular grouping of days into units came to be known as the month. The grouping of days into units smaller than a month varied widely from culture to culture. The most popular grouping of months together came to be known as the year.

They also faced the problem of when the units of time should begin, when they should end, and against what natural events time should be measured: 'moon', 'sun', or 'star' time?

MEASURING THE DAY

How long should a day be? It seems that the ancient priest-astronomers universally, even though quite independently, decided that a day should include one period of light and one period of darkness, but they did not agree on when a day began. The ancient Babylonian, Egyptian, Chinese and Hindu priest-astronomers decided to measure a day from sunrise to sunrise. The ancient Hebrews decided to measure a day from sunset to sunset. The ancient Umbrians (a province in central Italy) decided to measure a day from noon to noon, while the ancient Romans decided to measure a day from midnight to midnight.

There was also a wide variety of ways to divide a day into smaller units. In ancient Egypt it was the custom to divide the day into twelve equal parts from sunrise to sunset and into twelve equal parts from sunset to sunrise. This resulted in a daylight 'part' at the summer solstice being seventeen minutes longer than our standard hour of 60 minutes. In ancient Sumeria, the day was divided into six watches (standard periods of time for keeping guard), three during daylight and three during the night. The length of the watches varied with the season. Early Christians seem to have used both methods, dividing the day from sunrise to sunset into hours and the time from sunset to sunrise into watches. For example, in Matthew 14:25, there is a reference to the "fourth watch of the night".

Today, scientists measure the length of a day as 23 hours, 56 minutes and 4.1 seconds of mean solar time. However, it is standard practice in both eastern and western countries to divide the day into 24 parts, or hours, with each part containing 60 minutes. Some countries, such as France, consistently use a 24-hour clock, numbering from the one o'clock after midnight. In other countries, such as Canada, the United Kingdom, and the United States, the 12-hour clock is the norm. But even where the 12-hour clock is mainly used, it is a common practice for the military forces of the country to use a 24-hour one. For the sake of clarity, transportation timetables in some countries are always written using the 24-hour system.

In the modern world, there are still two ways used to determine when a day should begin. One is to begin a day at sunset and the other is to begin at one minute past midnight. Among the people who begin a day at sunset are those who use the Hebrew, Hijri and Badí' calendars, and among the people who begin a day at midnight are those who use the Julian and Gregorian calendars.

GROUPING DAYS INTO SMALL UNITS

In ancient times it was the custom in West Africa to group four days together, in China and India five days were grouped together and in Assyria it was six days. In ancient Rome an eight-day period was used to determine marketing days and in Egypt it was a ten-day period. In addition to using both five- and ten-day units, the ancient Chinese, Hindus and Teutons grouped fourteen days together, a custom that lives on today in the period some call a fortnight. In more modern times, the calendar adopted by the French revolutionaries in 1792 abandoned a seven-day week in favor of a grouping of ten days. And the Soviets, after the Russian Revolution, instigated a calendar that grouped five days together.

THE WEEK

The practice of grouping seven days together has been the most popular of all of the small groupings of units of time. This seven-day unit of time is known as a week. Some scholars believe the association of seven days in one group was influenced by the regular rhythm of the phases of the moon. It takes approximately, *but not exactly*, seven days between each phase of the moon. So in cultures where life was organized around the phases of the moon, the days of the month that were celebrated were not every seventh day but the first, eighth, fifteenth and 23rd days of each month.

Because the seven-day week is shorter than the moon phases, other scholars disagree with that theory. The regular observance of a seven-day week would soon be out of synchronization with the moon phases unless extra days were inserted. An alternative theory is that the grouping of seven days together was based upon the biblical story of Creation, as found in the Book of Genesis. Advocates of this theory believe that the seven-day week as a measurement of time had nothing to do with lunar time and perhaps was humanity's first effort to establish a world independent of nature. Other scholars believe that the rhythm of a seven-day week, centered around *Shabbat* (the Jewish Sabbath Day), is a uniquely Jewish contribution to world civilization.

MEASURING THE MONTH

What could be simpler than to measure a month from one full moon to the next full moon or from one new moon to the next new moon? But nothing is ever quite so simple. The priest-astronomers who observed the phases of the moon discovered that the length of time from one new moon to the next new moon was $29\frac{1}{2}$ days (see Illustration 3), not 28, 29, or 30 days. That was awkward. What do you do with a half day? The ancient Chinese and Jewish priest-astronomers solved the problem of what to do with the half day by adopting a system of alternating months of 29 or 30 days each.

Since measuring time in months depended on the phases of the moon, the question of when to begin a month also depended upon the moon phases. The Chinese priest-astronomers decided that a month would begin with the sunrise immediately before a new moon.

THE WEEKEND

In 1889 Miss Braddon, a British novelist, wrote in *Day Will Come*, "Theodore and his friend betook themselves to Cheritan Chase on the following Friday, for that kind of visit which north country people describe as 'a weekend'."

The forty-hour, five-day work week became common practice in parts of the United States in the 1930s, but many workers still worked a half day on Saturdays into the 1950s. Today, the concept of the two-day break from work for many people on a Saturday and Sunday is fairly universal in North America and most of Europe.

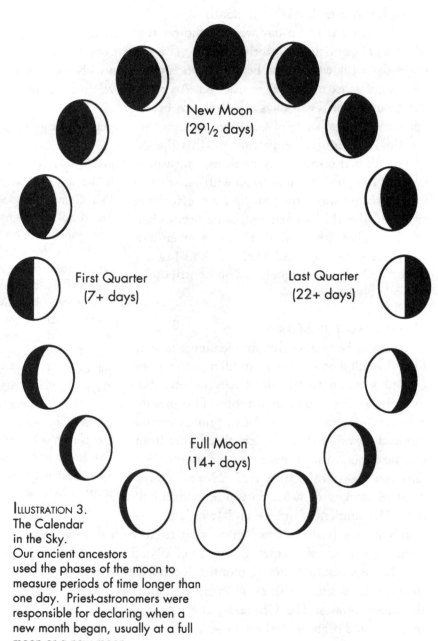

New Moon
(29½ days)

First Quarter
(7+ days)

Last Quarter
(22+ days)

Full Moon
(14+ days)

ILLUSTRATION 3.
The Calendar
in the Sky.
Our ancient ancestors
used the phases of the moon to
measure periods of time longer than
one day. Priest-astronomers were
responsible for declaring when a
new month began, usually at a full
moon or a new moon.

The Hindus chose to begin a month with the full moon. The Hebrews began a month at the first sighting of a crescent new moon. Later, Muslims were instructed in the Qur'án to begin a month from the time a new moon could be seen by the naked eye. When the ancient Romans balanced the lunar year with the solar year, they decided to begin a month at a fixed time and added one or two days to some of the months. As a consequence, the Roman months soon fell out of phase with the moon.

MEASURING THE YEAR

The priest-astronomers who were creating calendars needed to decide how many days, weeks and months to include in a year. The ancient star-watchers knew from observations that seasonal changes occurred regularly when a certain star, or stars, appeared in the sky. For example, Egyptian priest-astronomers decided that there were 365 days between the first appearance of the star they called Sothis, which we call Sirius, and the next time it appeared in the sky. The length of time from its first appearance to the beginning of its next appearance was called a sun (or solar) year. Gradually the records kept by the priest-astronomers did not match the reappearance of Sirius. They then realized that the sun year was actually slightly longer than 365 days, calculating that this was too short by about a quarter of a day. How could they incorporate a quarter of a day into their system? Here was another dilemma.

The priest-astronomers observed that there were twelve full moons from the appearance of certain stars until their next appearance. It was, therefore, convenient to group twelve moon months together and call that period a year. The majority of the world's calendars have twelve months in one year. There are two major exceptions to that practice, the Mayan calendar, which contains

ONCE IN A BLUE MOON

When two full moons occur in one month, the second one is called a Blue Moon. The expression 'once in a Blue Moon' means a very long time, probably because the occurrence is relatively rare. The time from a month with two full moons until the next month with two full moons ranges from a little less than two-and-a-half years to three years. A Blue Moon appeared in July 1985, May 1988, December 1990 and again in September 1993.

eighteen months of twenty days each, and the Badí' calendar, which contains nineteen months of nineteen days each. Both of these calendars use a system of intercalary days to balance the calendar with the solar year.

OBSERVATIONS AND RIDDLES

The use of the number twelve in timekeeping is interesting. Some scholars believe the use of the number twelve and multiples of twelve may have been influenced by the ancient Babylonians. The Babylonians believed twelve to be a mystic number. They based their measurements on multiples or divisions of twelve. They divided their day into 24 parts (2 x 12), an hour into 60 minutes (5 x 12), and a minute into 60 seconds (5 x 12). They also divided a circle into 360 degrees (12 x 30).

The days come and go like muffled and veiled figures sent from a distant friendly party, but they say nothing, and if we do not use the gifts they bring, they carry them as silently away.

– Ralph Waldo Emerson, Journals

Over the years, the observations of the priest-astronomers had shown them that nothing was as precise as they would have liked. A day was slightly less than 24 hours, a month was 29½ days long, a lunar year was slightly longer than 354 days and a solar year was slightly longer than 365 days. Their observations had also shown them that the beginning of a moon (lunar) year gradually fell behind the seasonal changes of the sun (solar) year. The ancient priest-astronomers of different cultures met these and other challenges of designing a calendar by devising some quite clever, unique, and sometimes complicated ways of measuring time and of organizing it into convenient units. Some of these methods became quite widespread and are still used, while others have been superseded by newer systems.

In addition to solving the riddle of how to measure a year, the priest-astronomers also had to decide when to begin a year. Should it begin in the spring, the autumn, the summer or the winter? In countries where the climate was hot and dry and where there were two rainy seasons, there were two periods of the renewal of life, and it became the custom to celebrate two new year's days in these countries. To avoid shortening the year, one new year's day was a civil celebration and the other a religious one.

BEGINNING DATES

Another decision the priest-astronomers had to make was what date should be used to mark the beginning of recorded time for their calendar. The beginning dates for the Hebrew, Julian, Hijri and Badí' calendars were all determined by an extraordinary religious event. The date used to mark the beginning of time for the ancient Roman calendar was the accepted legendary date for the founding of the city of Rome. That date is also particularly important to Christians because Dionysius Exiguus, an early Christian scholar, calculated the time of the birth of Jesus Christ from that date. In the sixth century, he suggested that time be reckoned from the birth of Christ and calculated that date to be 753 years after the founding of Rome. Unlike this well-documented chronology, unique events used to fix the beginning dates of most early calendars have been lost in history.

A common method for counting years in some countries has been to count the years from the beginning of the reign of a king or queen. Some nations still date certain things from the beginning of the reign of their current monarch. For example, in the United Kingdom the Acts of Parliament are dated from the year marking the beginning of the reign of the ruling king or queen, and in Japan coins are dated from the year marking the beginning of the reign of the current emperor.

RELATING DATES

For thousands of years different nations and cultures felt no need to coordinate their methods of reckoning time or of calculating dates with other nations and cultures. This has made it difficult for scholars to relate the dates of significant events in one culture to those in another. When the Christian chronicler Dionysius Exiguus proposed the use of the term Anno Domini in describing dates, his proposal enabled Christian scholars to compare historic events in other cultures as having occurred before or after the date Dionysus Exiguus had fixed as the birth date of Jesus Christ. Thus it became customary for dates to be given with the initials AD, for Anno Domini (the year of our Lord), or BC, for Before Christ, when dating events in history.

When some non-Christian nations adopted the use of the Gregorian calendar, they preferred to indicate dates with initials that would not be associated with Jesus Christ. It was decided to use CE, which stands for 'Common Era', in place of AD. Instead of using BC, they use BCE, which stands for 'Before the Common Era'.

SOME
INTERESTING
CALENDARS,
OLD & NEW

Mankind has long experimented with ways to measure and record time. Many methods have been relegated to history, but not all of them have been completely forgotten, especially some of the more ingenious systems. In this chapter we will take a look at a few of those experiments.

Where there is no vision, the people perish...
– Proverbs 29:18

CHINESE CALENDAR

No one really knows how old the Chinese calendar is. It was not the custom of ancient Chinese chronologists to number years consecutively from a single, fixed point. Their practice was rather to count years from the beginning of the reign of each new emperor.

A calendar day was measured from sunrise to sunrise. Days were usually counted in units of 60 but it was common to group days in smaller units of five or ten. It was customary to refer to an event as happening in the first, middle or last decade of a month. The days in the smallest unit, a group of five days, were named after the five basic elements thought to be the building blocks of the world: iron, wood, water, feathers and earth.

A calendar year was made up of twelve lunar months. To balance the lunar year with the solar year, an extra month was added seven times every nineteen years. An intercalary month was added during the summer when a month would begin and end in the same Zodiac sign. These so-called signs of the Zodiac were expressions of the imaginations of the ancient sky-watchers and priest-astronomers. As observations were made about the movements of the stars, certain groups of stars were described as resembling an animal or mythological figure and so named. Twelve distinct groups of stars were observed passing over a fixed point each year.

The new year began with the first new moon after the sun had entered the Zodiac sign of Aquarius, so it does not occur on the same calendar date each year. On the Gregorian calendar, the Chinese New Year's Day can occur any time between 20 January and 19 February.

The Chinese did not give names to the twelve months. They referred to a month by number, that is first month, second month, third month and so on.

They did, however, name the years in groups of twelve and it is still the custom to refer to a year by its name. The names of the years, in English, are: Rat, Ox, Tiger, Hare (Rabbit), Dragon, Snake, Horse, Sheep (Goat), Monkey, Rooster, Dog and Pig. The list of names is repeated in the same way that the month names are repeated on the Gregorian calendar. Groups of twelve years were arranged in cycles of 60 years.

Ancient Chinese records show that the science of astronomy was well developed in China. Observations of eclipses were reported, recorded, dated and interpreted as long ago as 1400–1200 BC. The records show that the Chinese used simple astronomical instruments such as gnomons for measuring time. A gnomon is a pillar or column-like structure that by the position or length of its shadow, as recorded at noon over a period of time, serves as an indicator of the hour of the day or the sun's meridian altitude. In north central China there was a gnomon about 2.5 meters high which cast a shadow of about 46 cm long when the sun was at its peak during the summer solstice. The ancient Chinese built a brick observatory tower in north central China at the city of Yang-chhêng. The twelve-meter high tower enabled the astronomers to make very precise measurements of the length of the solar year.

Research has disclosed that the tomb of the great Chinese Emperor Qin was aligned with the cardinal compass points of east, west, north and south. The inner and outer walls surrounding the burial mound also face the cardinal points. It was at this site that a fantastic discovery was made in 1974 on the east side of the burial mound. An entire army of life-size terracotta figures was uncovered. Because the tomb seems to be oriented to the north pole, archaeologists thought it was logical that there might be finds at the other cardinal points. A test dig in 1981 uncovered yet another remarkable discovery when two four-horse bronze chariots were found.

The Chinese calendar is still used in Tibet, Malaysia, Hong Kong and Singapore, but today it is mainly used for setting the dates of the traditional festivals, such as the Harvest Moon Festival and the New Year's Day Festival. The date for the traditional New Year's Day is now determined by the timing of the arrival of the new moon in the Far East.

MAYAN AND AZTEC CALENDARS

The ancient civilizations of the Maya and Aztecs in Middle America must have been linked at some point in their history. A strong indication that there was a cultural overlap and some interaction between these two great cultures is the fact that they share closely related calendar systems. Both the Mayan and Aztec calendars were divided into eighteen months of twenty days each with five intercalary days in regular years. Both had a 260-day sacred calendar meshed with an approximately 365-day secular one. Both used a complicated system of dating by combining a period of thirteen days with a period of twenty days. Both represented the days of the

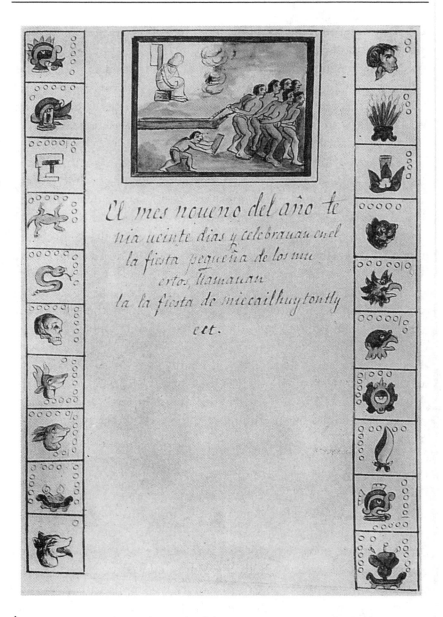

ILLUSTRATION 4. The ninth month of the Aztec year, *Miccailhuitontli*. A dead man is shown wrapped in his shroud on a seat, with a banner identical to the symbol for the number twenty, thought to be seen in the heavens at that time of the year, protruding from his back.

thirteen-day period numerically with dots and designated the twenty days of each month by name and glyph (a symbolic figure). However, the names and glyphs given to the days and the months by the Maya and Aztecs were not the same, even though both identified a date by its thirteen-day numerical position, its twenty-day name and a month name. The Mayan intercalary five-day period, sometimes referred to as a short month, was named *Uayeb*.

The Mayan and Aztec calendar systems may seem overly complex to us today but they were in fact very accurate methods of measuring time. The Mayan calendar dates back to a year corresponding to about 3300 BC according to Gregorian reckoning. The importance of that starting date has been lost because extremely few records of Mayan civilization survived the Spanish Conquest. It is known that they made accurate predictions of eclipses of both the sun and the moon and extensive observations of the movements of the planets. The Mayan priest-astronomers were highly skilled and their day-by-day studies enabled them to establish a calendar that very precisely followed the movements of the sun. To compensate for the year being a fraction of a day longer than 365 days, the Mayan priest-astronomers developed a very accurate formula for calculating a leap year to synchronize the calendar with the solar year, introducing this system more than 1000 years before the similar method developed by European astronomers.

The Maya's complex timekeeping system involved their short count (260 days) and long count (365 days) calendars running concurrently and meshing together much as a large gear and a small gear mesh together in a clock. The two calendars began on the same day only once every 52 years.

It is believed that the Maya named the days after local gods. For example there was *Imix*, the earth god; *Kan*, the corn god; and *Cimi*, the god of death. The day names sometimes varied from one area to another.

The Aztecs not only gave names to their days, they also assigned a special value to them, in a range from very favorable to unfavorable (see Table 1).

TABLE 1

Names of Aztec Days

DAY	AZTEC NAME	ENGLISH	VALUE
1	CeCipactli	Head of Serpent	good
2	Ehecatl	Wind	evil
3	Calli	House	good
4	Cuetzpallin	Lizard	good
5	Coatl	Serpent	evil
6	Miquiztli	Death	evil
7	Mazatl	Deer	good
8	Tochtli	Rabbit	neutral
9	Atl	Water	evil
10	Itzcuintli	Dog	good
11	Ozomatli	Monkey	neutral
12	Malinalli	Wild Grass	evil
13	Acatl	Reed	neutral
14	Ocelotl	Jaguar	neutral
15	Cuauhtli	Eagle	neutral
16	Cozcacuauhtli	Buzzard	good
17	Ollin	Motion	neutral
18	Tecpatl	Flint Knife	evil
19	Quiahuitl	Rain	evil
20	Xochitl	Flower	neutral

Transliteration and definition of these names come from Fray Diego Duran's *Book of the Gods and Rites and the Ancient Calendar*, the result of research undertaken by this Dominican missionary to Mexico in the late 1500s. This work was edited and translated into English in 1971 by Fernando Horcasitas and Doris Heyden (University of Oklahoma Press).

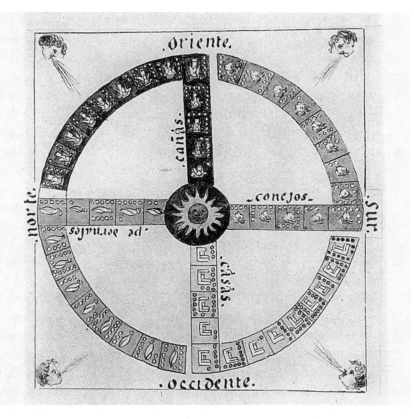

ILLUSTRATION 5. The Aztec cycle of fifty-two years, with four parts of thirteen years each, each quarter identified with a cardinal direction. East appears at the top.

Like the Mayan day names, there is a slight variation in Aztec names given to the days from one area to another. The five extra days needed to balance the year were considered particularly unlucky and were not given names, glyphs or numbers. They were referred to as *nemontemi*, or 'days left over and profitless'. The glyphs used to represent the days (and months) were a form of picture writing representing important events in Aztec history, or agricultural activities such as preparing the land for planting or the sowing of bean and squash seed.

The first day of each month was a solemn feast day on which no work was permitted. Even the food to be served had to be prepared on the previous day. Fray Diego Duran reported in the late sixteenth century that the natives observed the day 'rigorously'. The next division of time after the day, for both the Aztecs and Maya, was the period of thirteen days, of which there were 28 in a year. The first day of these periods was also a solemn feast day. On the calendar these periods were represented by dots, from one to thirteen. When thirteen was reached the counting began with one again, rotating through the series of symbols for the days.

The 52-year cycle was known as a Calendar Round to both the Maya and the Aztecs. The Aztec Calendar Round, as illustrated by Fray Diego Duran in his manuscript (see Illustration 5), was divided into four quarters. Each quarter was associated with a cardinal direction and contained thirteen years. The first part belonged to the east, the second to the north, the third to the west, the fourth to the south. The eastern quarter contained thirteen 'Years of Reeds', the northern quarter, thirteen 'Years of Flint Knives', the western quarter, thirteen 'Years of Houses', the southern quarter, thirteen 'Years of Rabbits'. Starting in the center of the circle at the sun symbol, one counts to the east and continues in a spiral, counter-clockwise motion – 1 Reed, 2 Flint Knives, 3 Houses, 4 Rabbits, 5 Reeds, 6 Flint Knives, 7 Houses, 8 Rabbits, and so on. When thirteen is reached the numbering begins at one again.

In addition to the solemn feasts held on the first day of each thirteen-day period and the first day of each twenty-day month, there was also a great ceremony held at the end of the cycle of the 52-year calendar round as well as the festivals held in honor of the gods and goddesses. Each feast or festival was celebrated with distinctive food, dances and games.

JALALI CALENDAR

Sometime about the year AD 1077, Omar Khayyam devised, with the assistance of a group of royal astronomers, a new calendar. Khayyam, who is better known in the West as a poet, was an accomplished astronomer and a minister in the court of the Sháh of Persia. The new calendar was called *Tarikh-i-Jalali* after the name of the reigning Sháh, Sultan Jelaledin. It was an extremely accurate calendar and while, for example, the Gregorian calendar is one day off in 3330 years, the calendar designed by Khayyam is off by only one day every 5000 years.

Like the old Zoroastrian calendar, the Jalali calendar had twelve months of 30 days each with five intercalary days added after the last month. But unlike its predecessor, the Jalali calendar had a system of leap years to keep the calendar balanced with the solar year.

IRANIAN SOLAR CALENDAR

Although modern Iran is a Muslim country, it does not use the strictly lunar calendar used by other Muslims. Instead, the year is divided into twelve months with the names of the months given in Farsi (the Persian language) rather than in the traditional Arabic of the Muslim Hijri calendar. Under the lunar Hijri calendar, new year's day rotates backwards throughout the seasons. In the Iranian calendar, the first day of the year always occurs at the vernal equinox, corresponding with the Gregorian date of 21 March.

The Iranian Solar calendar is also at variance with the Muslim Hijri calendar because it does allow the use of a system of intercalation to keep the calendar balanced with the solar year. It is still the official calendar of Iran.

A THIRTEEN-MONTH CALENDAR

In the mid-1800s, Frenchman Auguste Comte proposed a reformed calendar of thirteen months of 28 days each. This resulted in a year of 364 days exactly divided into 52 weeks. In common years, the intercalary day, named Year Day, was added and dedicated to the memory of the dead. In leap years, two intercalary days were added. Comte dedicated the second intercalary day to the memory of 'eminent women'. One of the most interesting aspects of Comte's calendar was his way of acknowledging contributions made to mankind. He named the days, weeks and months after the world's

TABLE 2

Names of French Revolution Months with Translation and Corresponding Gregorian Month Name

REVOLUTIONARY NAME (FRENCH)	(ENGLISH)	GREGORIAN (ENGLISH)
Vendémiaire	vintage	September
Brumaire	mist	October
Frimaire	frost	November
Nivôse	snow	December
Pluviôse	rain	January
Ventôse	wind	February
Germinal	seed time	March
Floréal	blossom	April
Prairial	meadow	May
Messidor	harvest	June
Thermidor	heat	July
Fructidor	fruits	August

great men and women. In all, his list contained 559 names of outstanding persons, representing what he felt to be the finest accomplishments of men and women in the history of mankind. Comte's calendar was a perpetual one – it always began on the same day of the week year after year.

CALENDAR OF THE FRENCH REVOLUTION

After the French revolutionaries overthrew their monarchy, the successful rebels wanted to make a fresh start and to celebrate and proclaim their newly won liberty by inaugurating a new calendar. A committee was appointed to do just that.

The committee decided to employ the decimal system in the new design. Each month was divided into three periods of ten days, each called a decade. Each day was divided into ten hours and each hour into 100 minutes and each minute into 100 seconds. Such drastic changes made it necessary to create new dials for all the clocks. The French citizens found this new method of timekeeping very confusing and voiced their opposition so vigorously that the new government was forced to give up the decimal divisions about three years after the great experiment had begun.

In adopting the decade, the committee had abandoned the seven-day week and the names of the days of the week. They gave the days Latin numerical names: *Primidi, Duodi, Tridi, Quartidi, Quintidi, Sextidi, Septidi, Octidi, Nonidi,* and *Decadi.* The tenth day of each decade was declared a day of rest.

The committee retained a year of twelve months but renamed the months with descriptive names. New year's day was changed from the first of January to the day in September that coincided with the autumnal equinox.

An Englishman, amused by the French Revolutionary calendar, wrote the following verse to make fun of its use of topical names for the months:

Autumn – wheezy, sneezy, freezy.
Winter – slippy, drippy, nippy.
Spring – showery, flowery, bowery.
Summer – hoppy, croppy, poppy.

Since twelve months of 30 days each added up to only 360 days, it was necessary to add five intercalary days in common years to balance the calendar with the solar year. The intercalary days were named *Sans-culotides* in memory of the poor ragged peasants of Paris who had been called the *sans-culottes* (literally people without a pair of breeches). In leap years, six intercalary days were added at the end of the year. The extra leap year day was dedicated to sports.

The French Republican calendar was dated from 22 September 1792, the date the Republic had been proclaimed. This new calendar, like the time divisions, was very unpopular in France. It was also disliked by neighboring countries, because it made communication with France extremely difficult.

The new calendar rapidly fell into disuse, and was abandoned less than fourteen years after it was proclaimed. Two things in particular led to its downfall – its design and the committee's announced intention at its inception of challenging the influence of the Roman Catholic Church. The Pope opposed the change, particularly the committee's abandonment of the seven-day week. When Napoleon became the head of the French government he made a pact with the Pope, pledging to reinstate the Gregorian calendar in return for the Pope's recognition of Napoleon's authority over France.

U.S.S.R. REVOLUTIONARY CALENDAR

Like the French revolutionaries, the Soviets also strove to break the hold of the church, but in this case it was the Russian Orthodox Church. Unlike the French, the Soviets did not reform the calendar immediately after their revolution in 1918. Instead, the new government adopted the Gregorian calendar which, in a sense, rejected the Julian calendar, still the official calendar of the Russian Church. In 1929 the new government, still struggling to break the hold of the church, decided to reform the Gregorian calendar. The changes began with the abandonment of the seven-day week. A five-day week was created. There were four working days and one day of rest in each week, and six weeks in each month. In addition to these days of rest there were also extra holidays, with the five or six intercalary days needed to balance the calendar with the solar year declared to be holidays. The days of the week were numbered and not named, but the month names were retained. In 1932, the format of the months was changed. Instead of having six weeks of five days each, the new arrangement was to have a month of five weeks with six days each! All this tampering with the traditional seven-day week was just too radical for average Soviet citizens. They protested. The changes had proven to be too great an adjustment for them to make. Eventually the government of the U.S.S.R was obliged to give up its efforts to introduce calendar reform. In 1940 it officially abandoned the revolutionary six-day week and five-week month and adopted the Gregorian calendar once again.

WORLD CALENDAR

A more modern attempt at calendar reform is the World calendar. The names of the days and the months are the same as those used in the Gregorian calendar, but there the similarity ends. The year is divided into four equal quarters of exactly 91 days or thirteen weeks. Each quarter contains three months, one month of 31 days and two months of 30 days each. The year always begins on a Sunday and ends on a Saturday. Therefore it perpetually repeats itself. In common years an intercalary day is added after 30 December. It is designated as 'December W' and is considered either as a 'World Holiday' or as an extra sabbath day. In leap years, another inter-calary day is added after 30 June. It is also considered a 'World Holiday' or an extra sabbath day and is designated as 'June W'. It is the hope of the people who support the World calendar that the two 'W' days will help to promote greater world unity.

UNWRITTEN TIMEKEEPING SYSTEMS

*Man is the product
of his thinking. All
that he is, all his
ideals, likes and
dislikes, his very
self, is the result
of thought.*

– Buddhist
Scriptures

Some primitive peoples did not have a written language. This does not mean that they were unintelligent or had no desire to keep track of time. But how do you create a calendar when you do not have a written language? How do researchers learn about ancient timekeeping systems when there are no written records to guide them? Lack of a written language has made it very difficult to discover the ways in which primitive societies measured time and developed timekeeping systems. However, some progress is being made.

NATIVE NORTH AMERICAN SYSTEMS

It is believed that some tribes in North America kept a tally of the long dark days of winter on notched sticks. Others kept track of time by counting moons and gave them descriptive names. The Nootka people, for example, referred to the month we call March as 'Herring-spawn

Moon'. It was followed by 'Wild Goose Moon' a time when geese, ducks and other waterfowl were winging their ways along the Pacific flyway. The next month was called 'Getting-ready-for-Whaling Moon'.

Recording years was more challenging to the original inhabitants of North America than naming months. Some tribes designated past years by 'winter counts'. The Sioux recorded their tribal history by painting pictures representing each winter on a large hide. Each picture portrayed a special event that had occurred during that year. For example, the year 1834, called the 'Winter of Meteor Shower', was represented by a picture of meteors; while the year 1870, called the 'Winter of Solar Eclipse', was represented by a picture of an eclipse of the sun.

The greatest advances in studying the time systems of Native Americans have been accomplished by a new breed of scientists called archaeoastronomers. They are making fresh and exciting discoveries about how ancient civilizations measured time and kept track of dates. Archaeoastronomers, combining the disciplines of archaeology and astronomy, have shown that the native inhabitants of the United States made regular, skillful and accurate observations of the sun, moon and stars. This understanding has given new meaning to the ritual buildings some of the tribes built, and to the stone and wooden circles and large earth mounds that are the legacies of other tribes.*

NAVAHO SKY CALENDAR

It was the Spanish who gave the name Navaho to the inhabitants of the southwestern United States, but Dineh is the name they called themselves, a word that translates as 'the People'. Because the Dineh considered life itself as sacred, the sacred and secular times in their lives blended. They were ranchers rather than farmers, never settling in just one place, choosing one location for winter and another for

* For a wealth of detail and examples of the remarkable understanding by the North American aboriginal nations of astronomy, see *Living the Sky – The Cosmos of the American Indian* by Ray A. Williamson (Boston: Houghton Mifflin, 1984).

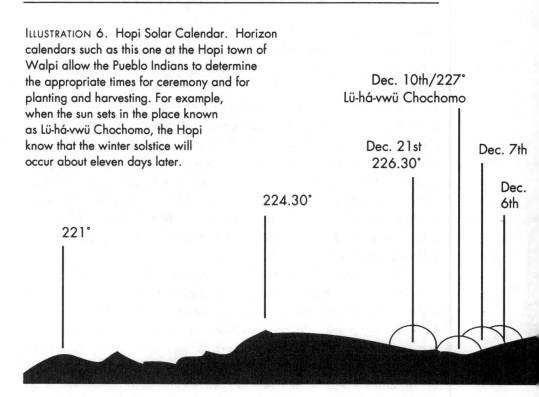

ILLUSTRATION 6. Hopi Solar Calendar. Horizon calendars such as this one at the Hopi town of Walpi allow the Pueblo Indians to determine the appropriate times for ceremony and for planting and harvesting. For example, when the sun sets in the place known as Lü-há-vwü Chochomo, the Hopi know that the winter solstice will occur about eleven days later.

Dec. 10th/227°
Lü-há-vwü Chochomo

Dec. 21st
226.30°

Dec. 7th

Dec.
6th

224.30°

221°

summer. Because of this lifestyle, the Dineh depended upon the stars and their movements to set the times for special events. If they had relied upon the position of the sun or moon, they would have needed a fixed horizon from which to make observations, so, as a nomadic people, the movement of the stars was a more appropriate calendar for them. By observing the positions of the constellations, the Dineh skywatcher could take his calendar with him as he traveled.

The Dineh believed 'Black God' placed the stars and constellations very carefully in the sky and gave them their names. Black God's star patterns remained in groups and moved about the sky in a regular rhythm. Certain Dineh, who were given the responsibility to watch the movement of these constellations, became very skillful at reading the calendar in the sky, skills that were vital to the success of their dry farming techniques.

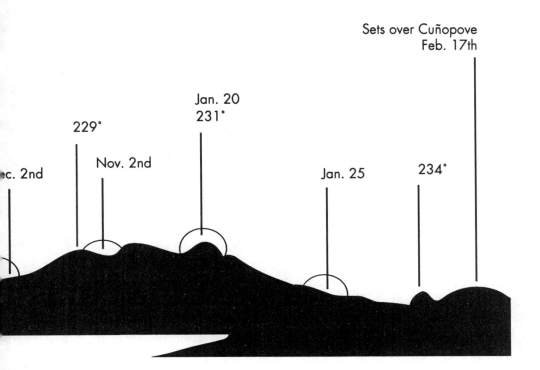

Even the building of the hogan, the traditional Dineh house, was influenced by the cardinal compass points in its position and design. In the common five-log hogan, major supporting logs were placed in the south, west and north corners. The doorway, which always faced east, was framed by two smaller logs. Because the hogan's beauty was derived from its cosmic plan, no decorations were added to either the inside or the outside of the dwelling. To decorate it would have implied that the cosmic plan was not beautiful enough.

PUEBLO SUN-PRIESTS
Those who lived in fixed pueblo settlements, such as the Zuñi and Hopi, had sun-priests. The Zuñi sun-priest, as described by

Williamson, used an observation method based on the position of the sun along the horizon at dawn. This was combined with further observations needed to set the day when spring planting should begin. By watching the alignment of the shadows of an outcropping on Corn Mountain (the Zuñi sacred mountain) and a man-made column, he knew when it was time to prepare the fields.

The Hopi sun-priest observed the places on the horizon where the sun set and became very familiar with these landmarks. The landmarks were given specific titles much as constellations are given names. The system they developed is known as a horizon calendar. Through use of the horizon calendar, the sun-priests were able to predict quite accurately when the winter and summer solstices, and the spring and autumn equinoxes would occur.

As well as being extremely important to the pueblo dwellers for agricultural reasons, the horizon sightings also had deeply religious significance, since the timing of their major religious ceremonies depended on the solstices and equinoxes. For example, in the western pueblos the *Kachina* cult ceremonies began one month before the winter solstice and lasted until one month after the summer solstice, the timing being completely dependent upon accurate horizon sightings.

A more ancient pueblo people, called the Anasazi, are known to have observed the summer solstice sunrise at a site near Holly House, Colorado, in what is now Hovenweep National Monument. Here a narrow corridor, about $5^1/_2$ meters (18 feet) long, is formed by two large boulders, opening toward the eastern horizon. At the summer solstice there is a display of sunshine and shadow in the corridor. Streaks of light, caused by the sun and the complicated shape of the boulders, create two serpent-like light shapes on the face of the southern boulder. This phenomenon was recorded by the Anasazi using carved glyphs on the boulder. A sun-priest, using this natural phenomenon and the glyphs as a calendar, was able to predict dates quite accurately.

In the years between AD 800 and 1000, the Anasazi built towers and houses with blocks of sandstone, bits of mortar and adobe plaster,

SUMMER
SOLSTICE
SUNSET

WINTER
SOLSTICE
SUNSET

EQUINOX
SUNSET

· FLOOR PLAN ·
NOT TO SCALE

ILLUSTRATION 7. Hovenweep Castle Sun Room. The solar observing room in Hovenweep Castle in Colorado. Two ports and a doorway define a complete solar calendar.

the ruins of which are also located at Hovenweep. These buildings, with their carefully positioned small windows, were also used to help measure time and predict dates.

The largest surviving tower at Hovenweep contains what can only be described as a solar calendar room. The four major events of the solar year, the solstices and equinoxes, are measured there. The equinox alignment occurs between the inner and outer doorway uprights and the eastern inner doorway (see Illustration 7). At sunset on the winter solstice, a beam of light shines through a small window and falls on the east corner of the doorway leading into another tower (D tower). In addition, the west edge of the exterior doorway casts a shadow to the east upright of the door to D tower. As the sun continues its way back north, the beam of light passing through the small window falls gradually further east on the wall until it finally disappears. Experiments in dating the timbers in D tower indicate that it was built about AD 1166. The towers at Hovenweep and their complex features are a continuing testimony to the extraordinary skills of the Anasazi as timekeepers.

AUSTRALIAN ABORIGINE SKY-WATCHING

The Australian Aborigines had little need for a sophisticated calendar to measure time precisely, because as hunter-gatherers they did not engage in agricultural activities. They were concerned primarily with the past and present and showed little interest in predicting the future. Awareness of time meant being familiar with the position of the sun, the moon or specific stars in relation to natural events such as the ripening or appearance of seasonal food, or the beginning of good or bad weather.

For example, one tribe in south-eastern Australia knew that when they observed the star they called Marpeankurrk (Arcturus) in the north at evening, it was time for them to gather the larvae of the wood-ant, a prized delicacy. And when Marpeankurrk set with the sun, they knew the season of the larvae was over. The tribe believed that Marpeankurrk had been one of their ancestors and it was she who had first discovered the larvae. When she died, she made herself into a star to help her people remember when the larvae would be in season.

A tribe in eastern New South Wales named the constellation known as Pleiades, the 'Seven Sisters'. When they observed the 'Seven Sisters' setting with the sun it was thought that the sisters had gone away to bring winter. When the 'Seven Sisters' reappeared in the eastern sky, the aborigines knew that the warm weather was on its way. Another tribe marked the onset of the wet and dry seasons by observing the position of the constellation we call Scorpio. They also judged the arrival of seasonal birds and game by watching for the appearance of Orion, Pleiades and the Southern Cross.

So, while the positions of the stars in the sky may not have concerned the aborigines for agricultural reasons, in the timing of the gathering of food the stars were vital. For some, the proper time for hunting termites coincided with the position of Arcturus on the horizon in the evening, while for others the best time to find the eggs of the Mallee hen was when they observed the appearance of Vega. The tribes of the native peoples of Australia developed their skills as sky-watchers in order to survive as hunter-gatherers in the often harsh climate of their homeland.

WESTERN EUROPEAN STONE CIRCLES

The ruins of hundreds of pre-Christian era stone circles are scattered around the British Isles, France and other parts of Western Europe. Some are believed to date back to neolithic times around the third millennium BC, and others to the Bronze Age. Many books have been written and theories propounded about the origins and meaning of the stone circles, but the very construction of these circles, some small and some of enormous proportions, indicates the finely tuned skills of our ancestors.

According to archaeologist Colin Renfrew, the British stone circles had three features: they were geometrically precise, there was a specific relationship between the number of stones in a circle's circumference and the length of the diameter of the circle, and they

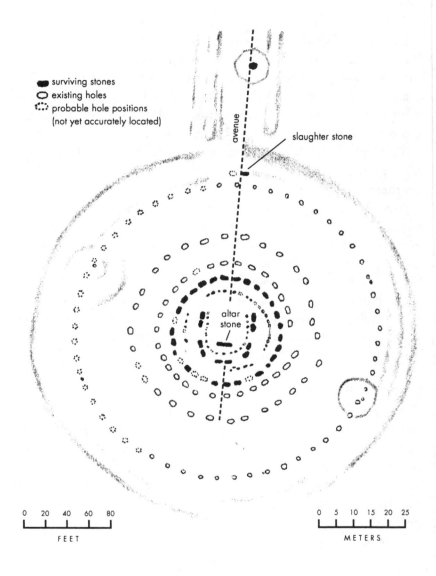

- ● surviving stones
- ○ existing holes
- ⦂⦂⦂ probable hole positions
  (not yet accurately located)

avenue

slaughter stone

altar stone

| 0 | 20 | 40 | 60 | 80 |
FEET

| 0 | 5 | 10 | 15 | 20 | 25 |
METERS

ILLUSTRATION 8. A plan of Stonehenge as seen from above showing the alignment of the sun at dawn on the summer solstice (dotted line).

appear in many cases to have astronomical alignments relating to the moon and the sun at the time of the solstices.*

The most famous of all stone circles is Stonehenge. Dates for the construction of this English stone circle vary from 1900–1600 BC back as far as 3000 BC, making it, at Colin Renfrew's estimation, the "world's oldest astronomical observatory".

It is generally agreed that this imposing monument is unlike any other stone circles, the majority of which in Western Europe appear to be tombs, while Stonehenge has long been recognized as an accurate observatory used as a dependable calendar for predicting the seasons.

The butterfly counts not months but moments, And has time enough.

– Rabindranath Tagore, Fireflies

Located on a fairly level plain near Salisbury in Wiltshire, Stonehenge is an awe-inspiring structure. Beginning at the outer edge, there is a ditch that encircles the site, which is 97.5 meters (about 320 feet) in diameter. A bank of earth, chalk and gravel is piled on the inside edge of the ditch. Next comes a circle of 30 sarsen (a type of natural sandstone) uprights, each pair of sarsens being joined at the top by a lintel. Then comes a bluestone circle. Next are five megalithic 'trilithons' of sarsen arranged in a horseshoe shape. A trilithon is made up of two precisely trimmed stones, topped by a lintel. At the center is a small bluestone horseshoe shape. To the north-east there is a break in the bank and ditch that is about 10.5 meters (about 35 feet) wide, called the causeway. The causeway leads to the 'Heel Stone', a single upright sarsen that stands about 30 meters (about 95 feet) down the causeway. The Heel Stone is unlike the other sarsen megaliths because it has no scars indicating chipping or scraping, while the sandstone slabs that make up the other megaliths show signs of being carefully prepared, shaped and smoothed.

Between the inner bank and the sarsen ring are three rings of holes, the outer circle of 56 regularly spaced Aubrey holes (named in

* *Before Civilization* by Colin Renfrew (Alfred A. Knopf, New York, 1973, pages 237–239).

honor of John Aubrey who described them in 1666) and inner circles of 30 'Y' and 29 'Z' holes. The number of Aubrey holes is believed to relate to a cycle of lunar eclipses which follow a pattern adding up to a total of 56 years. The numbers of holes in the Y ring and in the Z ring suggest that the holes were devices for measuring the days of the month.

It is believed that the rising of the winter moon was observed at Stonehenge by priest-astronomers to help them predict eclipses not only of the moon, but also of the sun. The occurrence of an eclipse must have been a very frightening experience for ancient peoples. A priest-astronomer who could accurately predict their occurrence was a powerful person indeed.

In addition, experiments have shown that the horseshoe of sarsen trilithons is oriented to the midsummer sunrise. In 1963, Gerald Hawkins conducted extensive tests at Stonehenge that suggested the monument was aligned not only with the midsummer sunrise, but also with other solar and lunar events. Hawkins suggests that the sun–moon alignments were created as a calendar for planting crops and to help create and maintain priestly power. At the conclusion of his tests at Stonehenge Hawkins remarked: "I think I have demonstrated beyond reasonable doubt that the monument was deliberately, accurately, skillfully oriented to the sun and the moon."*

When a British Government official was asked about Hawkins findings, he said, "I've heard about those findings but I don't believe them. You see, the ancient Britons couldn't have been as clever as all that." Hawkins' response was, "Actually, between 6000 and 2000 BC men in various parts of the world had invented and put to use the plow, the wheel, the inclined plane, the sailboat, the lever, the arch, the processes of loom-weaving, pottery-making, copper-smelting, glassmaking and beer-brewing, to name but a few of the many evidences of 'cleverness'."

* *Stonehenge Decoded* by Gerald S. Hawkins (Doubleday and Company, Inc. Garden City, 1965).

CHAPTER

CALENDARS OF SOME ANCIENT RELIGIONS

HINDU CALENDAR

India is a very large country with many ancient civilizations and calendars. At one time there were as many as seventeen different calendar systems being used to fix the dates of religious holidays. In 1957 the new Republic of India decided to simplify matters by adopting the Hindu calendar to establish the dates of religious holidays, and the Gregorian calendar for official and civil purposes.

The ancient Hindu calendar is the one used today for setting Hindu religious dates not only in India, but also in other places where Hinduism is practiced. No records have been found as yet to identify the extraordinary event that might have been used to fix the beginning of time for this calendar. It is known, however, that the Hindu priest-astronomers measured the day from sunrise to sunrise. Days were not grouped together into units as small as the

True to his holy law, he knows the twelve moons with their progeny; He knows the moon of later birth.
– Rig-Veda
1.25.8

seven-day week, but it was common to group days in units of ten.

The Hindu calendar system combined solar and lunar time reckoning. The *Rig-Veda* (ancient Hindu scriptures) contains the earliest known Hindu reference to a calendar year of twelve lunar months of thirty lunar days each. The lunar month, governed by the waxing and waning of the moon, was divided into two parts of fifteen days each. The first half began with the full moon and the second with the new moon. Not surprisingly, the first half was called *suklapaksa*, meaning the bright half, and the second, *krsnapaksa*, meaning the dark half. Each day of a fifteen-day period was named by a numeral, that is one, two, three, and so forth.

The names of the months and their corresponding Gregorian times are:

1 *Caitra* (March–April)
2 *Vaisakha* (April–May)
3 *Jyaistha* (May–June)
4 *Asadha* (June–July)
5 *Sravana* (July–Aug.)
6 *Bhadrapada* or *Prausthapada* (Aug.–Sept.)
7 *Asvina* or *Asvayuja* (Sept.–Oct.)
8 *Karttika* (Oct.–Nov.)
9 *Margasirsa* or *Agrahayana* (Nov.–Dec.)
10 *Pausa* or *Taisa* (Dec.–Jan.)
11 *Magha* (Jan.–Feb.)
12 *Phalguna* (Feb.–March)

While in northern India a month was measured from one full moon to the next full moon, in southern India a month was measured from one new moon to the next new moon. Special ceremonies were organized to celebrate the appearances of the new moon and the full moon. By tradition, a two-day festival marked the appearance of the new moon but only a one-day festival was held to mark the appearance of the full moon.

The solar month did not have a fixed number of days, but rather was astronomically fixed. It would begin when the sun entered one of the twelve zodiac signs. The length of time that the sun takes to travel from one sign to the next varies from 27 days during the shortest winter month to 32 days during the longest summer month. It was believed that a new month could not begin until the sun had entered the next sign.

The two systems (lunar and solar) were synchronized by adding an extra lunar month. The leap month was added when necessary after the month of *Asadha* or the month of *Sravana* and was called either *Dvitiya* (meaning second) *Asadha* or *Dvitiya Sravana*. In some areas, time was divided into five-year cycles with the years dedicated to the divinities of Fire, the Sun, the Moon, Creation and *Rudra* (the god *Shiva* when angry). In these places an extra month was added only in the second and fifth years of each cycle.

Major Festivals and Holy Days

In ancient India the calendar year was divided into six seasons: spring, summer, the rains, autumn, winter and the season of dew and mist. Later the year was divided into only three seasons: heat, rain and cold. A special festival was held at the close of winter to honor all of the gods, another at the beginning of the rainy season to honor the god of water and one at the beginning of autumn in honor of the first fruits. These seasonal feasts usually involved animal sacrifice, eating, drinking (sometimes of intoxicants), games and music. Special music was associated with each solstice. For example, drums were used to imitate thunder at the summer solstice. Hindus still celebrate the advent of spring, the new year and the coming of autumn.

Holi, the joyous spring festival, is usually celebrated for three days and includes pilgrimages to holy places, great bonfires, processions led by elephants to the sound of drums and conchs, and wonderful fairs. The shops sell sweet cakes, flower garlands, mangoes, sugar candy and cooked rice. During the merry street dances, people throw red and yellow water or powders on passers-by and, in general, enjoy uninhibited personal behavior.

Pilgrimages provide a serious side to Holi. For devout Hindus, the main purpose in making a pilgrimage to holy places is to offer penance for misdeeds, and to make or to renew vows. Vows are an important aspect of a Hindu's life. In addition to seeking forgiveness the pilgrim might ask for a favor or a change in fortune. Often, in making or renewing a vow, the devotee would circumambulate (walk around) the holy site. For participants, the ultimate benefit of performing a pilgrimage is a feeling of true spiritual happiness.

Diwali, the Hindu festival of light, celebrates jointly the victorious return of Lord Rama after defeating the demon king Ravana; the annual visit of Lakshmi, the goddess of good luck and prosperity; and the Hindu new year. Devout Hindus consider this festival a time of spiritual rebirth, when anger and sorrow can be put aside and the soul cleansed. The date of Diwali, set yearly by astrologers, occurs on the fifteenth day of the first half of the month of Karttika (October–November) at the new moon, the time when, it is said, Lakshmi leaves her heavenly abode to visit earth. During the festival, many Hindus still like to decorate their homes with rows of *diya* (small oil lamps and candles) to symbolize the brightness of a good spirit in a world darkened by sin and sorrow, and as beacons to guide Lakshmi to their homes in the hope that she will bring them good fortune in the coming year.

BUDDHIST SYSTEMS

Early Buddhists adopted the old Hindu calendar and adapted it to their own needs much as the early Christians adopted the Julian calendar and adapted it to their needs. At first, Buddhists seemed to observe the old system of six seasons, and later followed the custom of observing the three seasons of the old Hindu calendar.

The first Buddhist calendar grouped days into small units according to the phases of the moon. The days of the full moon and the new moon were observed with religious rites, and the days of the quarter moon were observed by fasting. In some areas a fast was kept not only on the days of the quarter moon, but also on the days of the full and new moons. These days were celebrated with clean garments and clean minds and hunting and fishing were forbidden. Trade and commerce were frowned upon on the fast days, and schools and courts of justice were closed. At the new year, a festival was held to celebrate the victory of light over darkness and the triumph of Buddhism over ignorance. The significant event used by many Buddhists to mark the beginning of time for their religious calendar is the death of Gautama Buddha.

As Buddhists migrated to other countries they gave up the Hindu calendar and adopted the calendar of the countries in which they settled. For example, in China, Buddhists arranged their festivals and fasts according to the Chinese calendar, while in Burma, Buddhists dated their calendar from 543 BC, the traditional date of the Buddha's earthly death and entrance into *nirvana*. In Tibet, a mixture of western and Chinese timekeeping was used. In Sri Lanka, it was the custom for each Buddhist monk to keep a personal calendar to keep track of the hours, days, lunar months and years since the death of the Buddha. In Japan, Buddhists used the Chinese calendar only until 1873, when they adopted the Gregorian calendar.

In many lands Buddhists continue to observe *Uposatha*, the fasts connected with the phases of the moon, and the various moral precepts and self-denials identified with these fasts.

Major Festivals and Holy Days

The three major festivals still observed by the majority of Buddhists are the birth of the Buddha (*Hanamatsuri*), His enlightenment (*Bodhi* Day) and His death (*Nirvana* Day).

Hanamatsuri, the flower festival, celebrates the birth of the Buddha. On this day a beautiful flower shrine is placed before the main shrine in Buddhist temples to remind the faithful of the Lumbini Garden in India where the Buddha was born and the time when, according to tradition, all the flowers in the universe burst into bloom. Bodhi Day celebrates the day on which Gautama Buddha meditated under the *bodhi* or banyan tree at the hour of dawn and was enlightened with supreme wisdom. Nirvana Day is the solemn observance of the death of the Buddha's earthly form and His entrance into *nirvana*.

Theravada Buddhists observe all three events on the same day, *Vesak*, which is the day of the full moon in the sixth month. *Mahayana* Buddhists who have adopted the Gregorian calendar observe the birth of the Buddha on 8 April, His enlightenment on 8 December and His death on 15 February. *Mahayana* Buddhists who have adopted the Chinese lunisolar calendar use movable dates rather than fixed ones for observing all three festivals.

ZOROASTRIAN CALENDAR

The Zoroastrians, who originated in ancient Persia, were well known for their skills in astronomy. Many scholars believe that the so-called three wise men who followed the brilliant star to Bethlehem in search of an infant king (see the Gospel of St Luke for the story of the three Magi and the infant Jesus) were Zoroastrian priest-astronomers. It is very difficult to date the beginning of the Zoroastrian calendar. Among religious scholars and historians, there is wide disagreement, but Zoroastrian tradition holds that Zoroaster (Zarathustra) lived between 660 BC and 583 BC. It is presumed that the calendar was developed soon afterwards.

The day was divided into five parts. In modern terminology these represented dawn to noon, noon to 3 or 4 p.m., 3 or 4 p.m. to twilight, twilight to midnight, and midnight to dawn. In the winter the period from noon to 3 p.m. was omitted and the early period was extended from dawn to the middle of the afternoon.

They divided the calendar year into twelve months of 30 days each. Each day was named for an attribute of God, with the first, eighth, fifteenth and 23rd days of each month being special days honoring the supreme deity Ahura Mazda (Ormazd). There is no evidence in the *Avesta* (Zoroastrian scriptures) that the early calendar divided the month into any smaller grouping of days. The months also were named after the attributes of God. On the few days when identical day and month names coincided, these days were declared to be *Jashan*, that is, holy days.

In common years, five days were added at the end of the year to help balance the calendar with the solar year. These days, considered

TABLE 3

Names and dates of *GAHAMBARS*

ANCIENT NAME	ENGLISH EQUIVALENT	GREGORIAN DATE
Maidyoi-zaremaya	Mid-spring	1–5 May
Maidyoi-shema	Mid-summer	30 June–4 July
Paitishahya	Bringing in Corn	12–16 September
Ayathrima	Homecoming (with herds)	12–16 October
Maidyairya	Mid-winter	31 December–4 Jan
Hamaspathmaedaya	Feast of Heavenly Souls	15–20 March

Traditionally, *Maidyoi-zaremaya* is the celebration of the creation of the sky, *Maidyoi-shema* the creation of water, *Paitishahya* the creation of earth, *Ayathrima* the creation of plants, *Maidyairya* the creation of animals, and *Hamaspathmaedaya* the creation of man. It is believed that the year may have been originally divided into seven months of summer and five months of winter, which may explain the variation in the intervals of the *gahambars*. Zoroastrians today celebrate the *gahambars* as times of charity and memorial commemorations.

sacred days, were named in honor of the five great divisions of the *Gathas*, hymns written by Zoroaster. The calendar did not have a leap-year system, but the priest-astronomers did know by their calculations that the year was approximately one quarter of a day longer than 365 days. As a result, the calendar lost one day every four years. To adjust for that time difference, they decided to add one month to the calendar once in every 120 years.

In addition to the year being divided into months, it also contained six shorter groupings of days called *gahambars*. The gahambar days are important festivals that some scholars believe celebrated the six periods traditionally associated with creation as

ILLUSTRATION 9.
Multifaith wall calendar showing the festivals and holy days of many faiths on a Gregorian calendar. The various faiths are represented by symbols.

mentioned in the *Avesta*. Table 3 shows the names and dates of the gahambars.

Major Festivals and Holy Days

Khordad Sal, the last day of the 'Feast of Heavenly Souls', celebrates three important events – the last day of winter, the day the Prophet

Zoroaster was born and the day of His revelation. *Naw-Rúz*, occurring on the vernal equinox, celebrates the renewal of life after the winter. The calendar year started at the vernal equinox, a practice that continues in Persia (now Islamic Iran) to the present day. *Zarthosht no diso* commemorates the day on which it is believed that Zoroaster died.

The festivals and holy days were all dedicated to God and were days of rest. Originally they were only one-day celebrations, but gradually were extended to five days. Because there is no recurring weekly day of rest in the Zoroastrian calendar, the people relied on the festivals and holy days to give them a break from their work. They celebrated by attending special ceremonies held at the temples, and by family gatherings to eat and offer hospitality to others in an atmosphere of love and joy.

THE HEBREW CALENDAR – THE CALENDAR OF THE JEWS

The beginning of time for Jews is the date traditionally accepted as the day of the Creation of the world as recorded in the Book of Genesis. Scholars are not in agreement about when the first written Hebrew calendar appeared, but it would be safe to say that its development can be attributed to both piety and political pressure.

It was vitally important to devout Hebrews, the ancestors of the Jews, to observe religious rites at the proper times. The sighting of the *Rosh Chodesh*, the new moon, marking the beginning of a new month was particularly important because it regulated the time of *Shabbat*, the Sabbath Day, and the dates for all festivals, holy days and fast days.

In Jerusalem the priests would climb the Mount of Olives and light a signal fire as soon as they had observed the crescent of the new moon. Their fire was the first in a chain of signal fires as

O come, let us sing unto the Lord ... Let us come before his presence with thanksgiving.
– Psalm 95:1

TABLE 4

Names of Babylonian & Hebrew Months

BABYLONIAN	HEBREW
Duzu	Tammuz
Abu	Av
Ululu	Elul
Tashritu	Tishri
Arahamnu	Heshvan
Kislimu	Kislev
Tebetu	Tevet
Shabatu	Shevat
Addaru	Adar
Nisanu	Nisan
Aiaru	Iyyar
Simanu	Sivan

Under the influence of the Jewish leader Rabbi Hillel II, Hebrew calendar reform began in AD 358. By the tenth century, calendar reform seems to have been completed and the calendar that was established was so accurate that it has not had to be adjusted since then. The Hebrew calendar today is exactly the same as it was centuries ago. In fact, it is the oldest of all calendars still in daily use for both religious and civil purposes.

Chronology of the Ancient World (second edition) by E.J. Bickerman (Cornell University Press, 1968).

priests, keeping watch on other summits in the distance, sighted the fire and lit their own signal. This process would continue until the news that the new month had been begun was sent by signal fires as far north as the city of Safed, about 225 km (140 miles) from Jerusalem. At one time the chain of signal fires extended like a telegraph system all the way to Babylonia. Faithful believers eagerly watched for, and relied upon, the signal fires so they would be able to observe their religious rites at the proper times.

1993 SEPTEMBER		ELUL 5753 - TISHREI 5754	אלול תשנ"ג - תשרי תשנ"ד	
SUNDAY **12**	Sunrise 6:33 זריחה Sunset 7:11 שקיעה	ערשטער טאג סליחות First Slichoth 26	כו 26	זונטאג
MONDAY **13**			כז 27	מאנטאג
TUESDAY **14**			כח 28	דינסטאג
WEDNES. **15**	Eve of Rosh Hashonoh 5754 Light Candles 6:46	ערב ראש השנה תשנ"ד זכור ברית עירוב תבשילין	כט 29	מיטוואך
THURSDAY **16**	1st Day Rosh Hashonoh Light Candles 7:53	ערשטער טאג ראש השנה תשנ"ד שופר, תשליך TISHREI	א 1	דאנערש.
FRIDAY **17**	2nd Day Rosh Hashonoh Light Candles 6:42	צווייטער טאג ראש השנה תשנ"ד שופר	ב 2	פרייטאג
SATURDAY **18**	Sabbath Ends 7:49	פ' האזינו, חפ' שובה ישראל (הושע י"ד) שבת שובה	ג 3	שבת

Daylight Savings Time   מולד תשרי: דאנערשטאג פרי 24 מינוט, 7 חלקים נאך 9.

ILLUSTRATION 10. A page from a Jewish pocket calendar in English showing the month of Tishri and corresponding Gregorian dates.

Imagine how distressed the people must have felt when it was discovered that enemies deliberately set false signal fires to trick them! And, to compound their distress, the Romans later prohibited the Jews from lighting any signal fires at all. The priests in Jerusalem then tried sending out special messengers with the news that the new moon had appeared, but because it took too long, a month could not be started everywhere at the correct time.

What could be done? The Hebrews were obliged to develop their own reliable written method of measuring time. It needed to be recorded so the priests and believers did not have to depend on signal fires or messengers. With a written calendar, the time of the new moon and the beginning of a new month could be shared by all the priests and believers.

The Hebrew priest-astronomers went to work. It is believed that the pre-Babylonian exile Hebrew calendar was a lunisolar one, but little else is known about it. Some scholars believe that the Hebrews began to use the Babylonian calendar about 586 BC and were much influenced by it. There certainly are similarities in some of the names of the months and in the basic design. If the Hebrews did adopt the Babylonian calendar, they seem to have added further important observations to its design resulting in a much more accurate method of measuring time. Significantly, the Hebrew calendar is still in use today while the Babylonian calendar has been relegated to the history books.

DAYS AND WEEKS

The Jewish day begins and ends at sunset, therefore its length varies with the seasons. It is believed that the Hebrews began the day at sunset because of the Bible verse, "And God called the light Day, and the darkness he called Night. And the evening and the morning were the first day" (Genesis 1:5). The calendar day is a 24-hour period measured from 6 p.m. to 6 p.m. at the meridian of Jerusalem. Each hour of the day is divided into 1080 parts called *chalakim*.

The Hebrew calendar week, which is a group of seven days, is a man-made measure of time. It is not governed by the natural rhythms of the earth, sun, moon or stars. It is believed to be based upon the story of Creation as told in the Book of Genesis. According to the story in Genesis, God created the world in six days and on the seventh day He rested. The Hebrews named the seventh day *Shabbat*, which means a day of rest. The Jewish Sabbath day, a day set aside to honor God, became the pivotal point around which Jewish life and worship revolved. The seven-day week became a constant measure of time that established the regular recurrence of *Shabbat*. It not only established a rhythm of life for the Hebrews and their descendants, but it has also affected the lives of millions of Christians and Muslims.

So great is the respect given by Jews to *Shabbat* that in years when a conflict with other Jewish festivals may occur, precedence is always given to *Shabbat*. It is also significant that the other days of the week are designated only by a number, that is, first day, second day, third day and so forth. The only day of the week deemed worthy of a name was the seventh day, the day of God, *Shabbat*.

TABLE 5

LENGTH OF HEBREW MONTHS

	MONTH	LENGTH
The Hebrews solved the problem	Nisan	30 days
of a lunar month being 29½	Iyyar	29 days
days long by alternating months	Sivan	30 days
of 29 and 30 days. The names,	Tammuz	29 days
order and length of the months	Av	30 days
are shown here.	Elul	29 days
There are twelve regular	Tishri	30 days
months in a common year.	Heshvan	29 days or 30
During a leap year, a thirteenth	Kislev	30 days or 29
month is added after *Adar*,	Tevet	29 days
which is given 30 days in a leap	Shevat	30 days
year. The leap month, called	Adar	29 days
Adar II, is given 29 days.		

THE SYNCHRONIZED YEAR

The Hebrew calendar synchronizes a cycle of lunar years with solar years. In each cycle of nineteen years there are twelve common years and seven leap years. The leap years occur in the third, sixth, eighth, eleventh, fourteenth, seventeenth and nineteenth years of the cycle. In ancient times, the observations of the priest-astronomers in Jerusalem determined the length of the years. Later, observation gave way to calculation in determining if a year was a common year or a leap year. The sequence of common and leap years became fixed after the acceptance of Hillel's reforms.

The number of days in a year can vary from 353 to 385 because, in addition to the reckoning of time, the Hebrew calendar is also influenced by religious requirements. In terms of year length there are six types: regular (354 days), deficient (353 days) and abundant (355 days) common years; and regular (384 days), deficient (383 days), and abundant (385 days) leap years. During a deficient year the month of Kislev is shortened by one day and during an abundant year the month of Heshvan is increased by one day.

The Heavens declare the glory of God; and the firmament showeth his handiwork.

– Psalm 19:1

The reason for this complicated variation in the length of a year is the problem of fixing the dates of two special holidays, *Yom Kippur* (Day of Atonement) and *Rosh Hashanah* (Jewish New Year). It is considered undesirable to have Yom Kippur, a fasting day, fall on the day before or the day after *Shabbat*, and it is forbidden for Rosh Hashanah to occur on *Shabbat*. The timing of the first day of Tishri (the start of the religious year) is controlled by changing the length of the year preceding that month. By adding or subtracting a day to the year prior to Tishri 1, the date of Rosh Hashanah is controlled for the following year. When a day is added to a year it is called an abundant year, and when a day is subtracted from a year it is referred to as a deficient year.

Nisan, the Passover month, still marks the beginning of the civil and agricultural year which, at one time, was determined by the ripening of the barley.

Calendar scholar Keith G. Irwin states that in common years, a year would begin on the first day of the week, the next year would begin on the second day of the week and the next on the third day and so forth. "After a leap year," Irwin says, "the starting day jumped over a weekday; the third-day beginning of that year, for example, would be followed by a fifth-day beginning for the next year. It was from this 'leaping-over' of a weekday that the leap year received its name."*

* For more detail see *The 365 Days* by Keith G. Irwin (New York: T. Y. Crowell, 1963).

Some Jews observe a grouping of seven years together, calling each seventh year a Sabbatical Year. In ancient times the year was commemorated by allowing the land to lie fallow, by setting slaves free and by cancelling all debts. A grouping of seven times seven years, which was known as a week of Sabbatical Years, was celebrated by a Jubilee Year. In addition to the same obligations as in the Sabbatical Year, there was the further obligation to restore property to its original owners. The Sabbatical Year lives on today through the custom of granting leave, with full or half pay, periodically (as every seventh year) to a person holding a professional position (such as a university professor) for traveling, research, or rest.

To accurately calculate the Jewish year that corresponds to a particular Gregorian year, it is usually necessary to use a conversion table. However, one can make a rough estimate by subtracting 1240 from the Gregorian year and then adding 5000.

Most of the methods for measuring the lapse of time have, I believe, been the contrivance of monks and religious recluses, who, finding time hang heavy on their hands, were at some pains to see how they got rid of it.

– William Hazlitt,
'On a Sundial',
Sketches and Essays

SOME SPECIAL DAYS

The Jewish new year's day, Rosh Hashanah (1 Tishri), ushers in a ten-day period ending on Yom Kippur. This period is devoted to recalling the creation of mankind, reviewing individual activities during the past year, offering prayers to God asking forgiveness for any wrongdoing committed, and petitioning God to restore harmony between individuals.

The Day of Atonement, Yom Kippur (10 Tishri), is the holiest and most solemn day of the Jewish religious year, devoted to prayer, fasting and the seeking of forgiveness for the sins one has committed during the previous year. The fast consists of complete abstinence from food and drink for a 24-hour period beginning at sunset on the eve of the Day of Atonement and ending on the Day of Atonement at sunset. Morning, afternoon and evening services are held in the synagogue, which is draped with white coverings as a symbol of purity.

Chanukah (25 Kislev–3 Tevet), the Festival of Lights and the Dedication of the Temple, is an eight-day period devoted to the remembrance of the famous victory of Judah the Maccabee over Syrian forces and Greek paganism, a triumph for religious freedom. After the battle, the Temple was rededicated and the oil lamp in it was lit. Although it only contained enough oil for one day, it burned for eight. Some families celebrate Chanukah by exchanging gifts, serving *latke* (potato pancakes), playing games with a *dreidel* (a spinning top) and lighting eight candles in a *menorah* (a special candleholder).

Pesach, or Passover (15–22 Nisan), is another very special eight-day festival. It is devoted to the commemoration of the dramatic flight of the Hebrews from slavery in Egypt. Jews recall the time when their ancestors were captives in Egypt, and the Pharaoh refused to allow them to leave. When an avenging angel was sent to kill the first-born child in each Egyptian household, the Hebrews were instructed to paint a sign on their doorways so the angel would pass "over the houses of the Children of Israel". The reason Pesach is sometimes called the Feast of the Unleavened Bread is because Jews eat only *matzoth* (unleavened bread) during the period of Pesach as a reminder of the unraised bread that their ancestors took with them as they hurriedly left Egypt.

CHAPTER

ANCESTORS OF THE GREGORIAN CALENDAR

CALENDARS OF ANCIENT GREECE

Ancient Greece did not have a unified calendar because each of her great city states had its own timekeeping system. It was not until Greece was conquered by the Romans in 87–84 BC that her civil affairs were uniformly governed by a calendar. Prior to the Roman conquest, the Greeks were influenced by the lunar calendars of Babylonia and Syria. The Greeks began the day at sunset, and began their year in the autumn at a time corresponding to the Gregorian date of 1 September.

The Attic calendar, used by some Greeks, was made up of a year divided into twelve months of 29 or 30 days each, plus an intercalary month of 29 or 30 days. The intercalary month was placed after the sixth regular month. At first, the extra month was intercalated every two years, but that made the year too long so occasionally it had to be omitted. It was then added

*Thy rays nourish
every garden;
When thou risest
they live,
They grow by thee.
Thou makest
the seasons.*
– Ancient
Egyptian
Scriptures

only on an irregular basis. The smallest unit of time, after the day, was a period of ten days. Each month was divided into three ten-day segments or decades. For the first two decades, the days were counted forward in sequence, being referred to as the first, second, or third day of the first decade. In the third decade the days were counted backwards from the end of the month.

The Athenians developed a lunisolar calendar. This was primarily to accommodate their religious needs, but it also subdivided the year by *prytanies*. A Prytany, a subdivision of the ruling Council, was on duty for a set term of days which also became known as a prytany. There were ten prytanies per year. When the lunisolar calendar came into use about the end the fourth century BC, documents were then dated by both the lunisolar calendar and the prytany system.

The year 264 BC saw the inauguration of the *Olympiad* dating system. It was made retroactive to 776 BC, which is traditionally accepted as the year when the games were first held. An Olympiad was the period of four years between the holding of the games, the beginning of any Olympiad dating from the first full moon after the summer solstice. This dating system fell out of favor in AD 440 after the 304th Olympiad.

EGYPTIAN CALENDARS

The most ancient Egyptian calendar was probably a lunar one devised in honor of the god of the moon and time, Thoth, and it was the influence of this ibis-headed god that determined the calendar's divisions. However, because it was difficult to balance the lunar with the solar cycle, the Egyptians later abandoned the lunar year and adopted a 365-day solar year. The priest-astronomers then divided the year into twelve months of 30 days each.

That left the problematic five extra days. These days were used to honor the bright, fixed star Sothis, known to us as Sirius, the appearance of which became the focus of the Egyptian timekeeping system.

An ancient Egyptian legend says that the goddess Isis became the star Sothis. As the star Sothis, the goddess was the mistress of the beginning of the year, and in fact, the Egyptian new year was determined each year by the reappearance of Sothis just before the sun rises near the time of the summer solstice. The legend says that Isis then entreats the Nile, personified as the god Osiris, to rise and flood the land with its fertilizing waters, keeping the desert at bay. Thus the skills of the priest-astronomers in 'reading' the sky enabled them to plan for the future. When they observed Sothis in the eastern sky at dawn, they could foretell the occurrence of the flooding of the mighty, life-giving River Nile, true to the legend.

The priest-astronomers' skills also influenced ancient Egyptian architecture. It is not known exactly how they made their measurements or what techniques were used, but the surviving ruins of their buildings are celestially aligned. There are records of an ancient Egyptian ceremony called 'Stretching of the Cord'. It was held before the construction of a new temple began. In the ceremony, the Pharaoh himself established the basic reference line for the orientation of the temple, probably in alignment with the constellation Pleiades, which ancient Egyptians knew as the Bull's Thigh. Each month would begin on the day when the waning crescent moon disappeared from the pre-dawn sky. Most of the days of the month bore the names of the feasts or priestly activities associated with them, giving evidence of the religious nature of the calendar.

A new calendar, based on solar time, was introduced after Upper Egypt and Lower Egypt were unified circa 3100 BC. The year was now exactly 365 days long, consisting of twelve months of 30 days each, plus five intercalary days. For the convenience of commerce, the month was divided into three ten-day periods. The religious calendar continued to use the rhythm of the moon for its ceremonies – intercalated as needed, to keep in time with the solar year. In 238 BC, when Egypt was under the foreign rule of Ptolemy Eugertes, there was an attempt to reform the calendar. An edict called for the addition of

TABLE 6

*D*EVELOPMENT OF THE ROMAN–GREGORIAN CALENDARS

ROMULUS 738 BC	NUMA 713 BC	JULIUS 47 BC	AUGUSTUS 8 BC	GREGORY XIII AD 1582
Martius 31	Januarius 29	Januarius 31	Januarius 31	January 31
Aprilis 29	Martius 31	Februarius 29–30	Februarius 28–29	February 28–29
Maius 31	Aprilis 29	Martius 31	Martius 31	March 31
Junius 30	Maius 31	Aprilis 30	Aprilis 30	April 30
Quintilis 31	Junius 29	Maius 31	Maius 31	May 31
Sextilis 30	Quintilis 31	Junius 30	Junius 30	June 30
Septembris 31	Sextilis 29	Julius 31	Julius 31	July 31
Octobris 30	Septembris 29	Sextilis 30	Augustus 31	August 31
Novembris 31	Octobris 31	Septembris 31	Septembris 30	September 30
Decembris 29	Novembris 29	Octobris 30	Octobris 31	October 31
	Decembris 29	Novembris 31	Novembris 30	November 30
	Februarius 28	Decembris 30	Decembris 31	December 31
303 days	355 days	365 days	365 days	365 days

a sixth day every fourth year to help harmonize the civil and religious system, but apparently the priests ignored this decree.

THE ROMAN SYSTEM

In Rome there was no separation of 'church' and 'state'. All activities, whether civil or religious, involved the Roman gods. Every action of the state and its citizens had to be carried out at times that met with the approval of the gods, as interpreted by the local priests. The priests were the guardians of the calendar. The calendar may have listed the days but it was the priests who decided what happened on any particular day.

The heavens call to you, and circle around you, displaying to you their eternal splendors, and your eye gazes only to earth.

– Dante, 'Purgatorio', 14, from The Divine Comedy

In Rome's earliest days, the calendar was lunar-influenced, yet had only ten months and 303 days in a year. It was not until the eighth century BC that the year was divided into twelve months. The names of the last four months of that original calendar, September, October, November and December, survive in common usage today.

For the Romans, reliance upon natural phenomena was not an accurate method for reckoning the passage of time because of the variation in weather conditions from season to season and from district to district. For example, some sheltered areas near Rome experienced an earlier spring. The movements of the constellations may have been excellent time systems for agriculture, but the stars were not the best of timekeepers when it came to measuring the month or the day.

As in other ancient or aboriginal cultures, the priests and wise men who were patient and skilled in observing the course of the sun, the phases of the moon and the movement of the stars were especially rewarded and given powers, privileges and responsibilities. One of the responsibilities was to announce the beginning of a new month. If a priest did not see the crescent moon, he postponed the beginning of a new month. And as it became necessary, he would balance the lunar year by adding one day three times every eight years.

Numa Pompilius, the second emperor of Rome (about 700 BC) added two months, January and February, to the old calendar. Numa's calendar became the calendar of the Roman Republic. This calendar, sometimes referred to as the pre-Julian calendar, was based on a year of 355 days. It had a somewhat different arrangement of days divided among the months. Four of the months (March, May, July, and October), were allocated 31 days, one (February) was given 28 days and the other seven were assigned 29 days.

It also had an unusual form of intercalation. In leap years the month of February was reduced to 23 or 24 days and was followed by an intercalary month of 27 days. Religious events that normally fell on the 24th or 27th day of February were held on the 23rd or 26th day of the intercalary month. The reasoning behind this unusual system of intercalation is now unknown. By assigning 31 days to some months, but only 27 days to the intercalary month, those responsible for designing the calendar broke away from a strictly lunar reckoning.

So far, we have been using Gregorian calendar month names for clarity. The latinized names of the Roman months were: *Januarius, Februarius, Martius, Aprilis, Maius, Junius, Quintilis, Sextilis, Septembris, Octobris, Novembris, Decembris.* The name given to the intercalary month was *mensis intercalaris.* Januarius and Martius were named after the gods Janus and Mars, who were honored during those months. The name Februarius comes from the verb *februare* which means to purify, as purification rites were held during that month. The source of the names for Aprilis and Maius is uncertain. The month of Junius was named in honor of the goddess Juno. The last six months were given names deriving from numbers, reflecting the position the months had held when the year was only ten months long.

Like the Greeks, the Romans divided the month into three sections but, unlike those of the Greeks, these sections were not equal. The dividing days occurred on the first day of the month, on the fifth day of short months or the seventh day of long months, and on the thirteenth day of short months or the fifteenth day of long months. The first dividing day was known as the *Kalends*, the second as the *Nones* and the third as the *Ides*, the English word calendar being a derivation of the Latin word Kalends. In each month, the Kalends was declared to be the day after the evening when the crescent moon was first sighted, the Nones was the day when the moon was observed in its first quarter and the Ides was the day of the full moon. Days were referred to, not by their position in the month, but by their position in relation to the part of the month in which they occurred; for example, the first day before the Nones, the fifth day before the Ides, the tenth day before the Kalends and so forth. It is a mystery why the Romans developed such a complicated system.

This familiar jingle was first published in 1606 in a play and later in 1635 in an Almanac.

Thirty days has September,
*   April, June and November*
All the rest have thirty-one
Save February
And that has twenty-eight
*   days clear*
And twenty-nine in each
*   leap year*

Julius Caesar was inspired to reform the Roman calendar after he had visited Egypt in 47 BC. On his return, he sought the advice of the Greek-Egyptian astronomer, Sosigenes. Caesar then declared that the year 46 BC would be 445 days long with an additional 23 days added at the end of February, and 67 days added between the months of November and December. That year became known as the 'year of confusion', but it did bring the calendar back into synchronization with the seasons. After this major adjustment, Caesar established a 365-day year intercalated by a leap-year day every fourth year. He also moved the beginning of the year from the first of March to the first of January. The months were lengthened to 30 or 31 days except for February, which was kept at 29 days in regular years and given 30 days in leap years.

It was at this time that the Roman Senate changed the name of the seventh month from *Quintilis* to *Julius* in honor of Julius Caesar. Later, the name of the eighth month was changed from *Sextilis* to

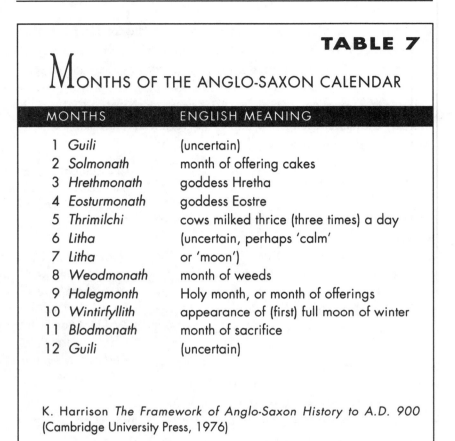

TABLE 7

Months of the Anglo-Saxon Calendar

MONTHS	ENGLISH MEANING
1 *Guili*	(uncertain)
2 *Solmonath*	month of offering cakes
3 *Hrethmonath*	goddess Hretha
4 *Eosturmonath*	goddess Eostre
5 *Thrimilchi*	cows milked thrice (three times) a day
6 *Litha*	(uncertain, perhaps 'calm'
7 *Litha*	or 'moon')
8 *Weodmonath*	month of weeds
9 *Halegmonth*	Holy month, or month of offerings
10 *Wintirfyllith*	appearance of (first) full moon of winter
11 *Blodmonath*	month of sacrifice
12 *Guili*	(uncertain)

K. Harrison *The Framework of Anglo-Saxon History to A.D. 900* (Cambridge University Press, 1976)

Augustus in honor of the Emperor Augustus, and, at his request, one day was taken from the month of February and added to the month of August so that the months of July and August would have an equal number of days.

THE SAXON CALENDAR OF PRE-CHRISTIAN EUROPE

Prior to the introduction of the Roman ecclesiastical calendar to England, the Saxon inhabitants had a calendar of which only remnants remain. It is known that the Saxon calendar was lunisolar with twelve lunar months adjusted occasionally to the solar year by adding an extra month in certain years. The calendar year began on 25 December shortly after the winter solstice.

The intercalary year was called *Thrilithi*. The thirteenth month was added in the summer, therefore there were three months called *Litha*. The first and last months also had the same name, *Guili*, which in Old English was *geol* and in modern English is yule. The term survives today in connection with Christmas festivities such as the burning of the 'yule' log and in wishing friends a happy 'yule' season. The name for the fourth month, derived from the name of the goddess Eostre, gave us the word 'Easter.'

Four weekday names that are in common usage in English-speaking countries – Tuesday, Wednesday, Thursday and Friday – were derived from the ancient Saxon calendar day names. And the Old English names – *Tiwesdaeg*, *Wodnesdaeg*, *Thunresdaeg* and *Frigedaeg* – were derived from the names of the Saxon gods Tiw, Woden, and Thor, and the goddess of fertility, Frigg.

Monday's child is fair of face,
Tuesday's child is full of grace,
Wednesday's child is full of woe,
Thursday's child has far to go,
Friday's child is loving and giving,
Saturday's child works hard for its living,
And the child that's born on the Sabbath day
Is bonny and blithe, and good and gay.   (Trad.)

THE JULIAN & GREGORIAN CALENDARS OF CHRISTENDOM

*Blessing, and
glory, and wisdom,
and thanksgiving,
and honor, and
power, and might,
be unto our God
for ever and ever!*

– Revelation 7:12

The Christian era begins with the date accepted as the year Jesus Christ was born. As the daily life of the early Christians was regulated by the Julian calendar of Rome, they adopted the Roman year of exactly 365¼ days, divided into twelve months, and retained the same names and lengths for each of the months. They did change the beginning date, counting time from Jesus' birth instead of from the founding of Rome. Another change made by early Christians at the time they adapted the Julian calendar to their needs was the introduction of a seven-day week. Their desire for a seven-day week was prompted by the Creation story and the need to celebrate the Sabbath. Yet, strangely enough, the names they gave to the days of the week seem to have been more influenced by pre-Christian Teutonic gods than by the Bible (see Table 8).

The Julian calendar was considered to be very accurate because the finest of the priest-astronomers of Rome had designed it under the authorization of Julius Caesar only fifty years before the birth of Christ. Therefore, the calendar the early Christians adapted to their needs had already been adjusted to bring the old lunar calendar into line with the solar year. Even so, it was not as accurate as had originally been hoped. It turned out to be eleven minutes and fourteen seconds too long per year. That may sound insignificant, yet that tiny error resulted in those few minutes adding up to *one whole day* every 128 years.

Over the years, the problem was discussed but no solution found. By AD 1582 the Julian calendar was ten days out of synchronization with the solar year, so Pope Gregory XIII ordered a study to be made on how the calendar could best be reformed. He recruited the most able scholars, priests, scientists and astronomers to conduct the study, which resulted in a calendar that measures time very accurately. The Gregorian reformers made

APRIL FOOL

The custom of playing tricks on friends and neighbors on 1 April is believed to have started over 400 years ago in France. Before 1564, under the old calendar used in Europe, the new year began on 1 April. It was the custom for people to exchange gifts and visit each other to celebrate the beginning of the new year.

Then in 1564 King Charles IX of France adopted the reformed calendar and decreed that the new year would begin on 1 January. Certain of his subjects did not like the idea of changing. They stubbornly continued to celebrate 1 April as New Year's Day. So, they became the target of jokes and tricks. Their friends and neighbors gave them mock gifts, invited them to fake parties and played all kinds of tricks on them – calling them April fools because they still observed New Year's Day on 1 April.

a minor, but exceedingly important, adjustment in calculating which years should be declared leap years. They decided that leap years should occur every four years *except for three of every four century years ending in 00.* For example, the year 1600 was a leap year. The years 1700, 1800, and 1900 were common years. The year 2000 will be a

TABLE 8

COMPARISON OF DAY NAMES

LATIN	FRENCH	SAXON (USAGE)	ENGLISH
Dies Solis	Dimanche	Sun's Day	Sunday
Dies Lunae	Lundi	Moon's Day	Monday
Dies Martis	Mardi	Tiw's Day	Tuesday
Dies Mercurii	Mercredi	Woden's Day	Wednesday
Dies Jovis	Jeudi	Thor's Day	Thursday
Dies Veneris	Vendredi	Frigg's Day	Friday
Dies Saturni	Samedi	Saturn's Day	Saturday

leap year. That subtle adjustment in the calculation of leap years is the key to the accuracy of the Gregorian calendar. This adjustment was all that was needed to create a valuable, accurate and reliable way of measuring time. In honor of Pope Gregory XIII, the reformed calendar was named the Gregorian calendar.

The Roman Catholic countries of Europe adopted the reformed calendar by the year 1587, five years after it was first declared by the Pope. Non-Roman Catholic countries were more reluctant to adopt a calendar that had been reformed under the auspices of the Roman Catholic Church and continued using the Julian calendar. It took the British Government 165 years before it finally adopted the Gregorian calendar in 1752, and this only after the calendar's name was changed to the New Style calendar to increase its acceptability.

At the time Pope Gregory XIII inaugurated the reformed calendar, it was necessary to drop ten calendar days. He declared that the day following 4 October 1582 would be known as 15 October 1582. Because the Pope had decreed it, Roman Catholics accepted the adjustment without question. It was not so easy in Great Britain. By 1752, when the British Parliament decided to adopt the New Style (Gregorian) calendar, the Julian calendar was eleven days out of synchronization with the solar year. It was necessary, therefore, for the British Parliament to decree that the day following 2 September 1752 would be known as 14 September 1752. The British people were furious. In England, some of the demonstrators against the government decree marched through the streets of London, shouting "Give us back our eleven days!"

The use of the New Style (Gregorian) calendar spread around the world quickly because the European nations imposed it upon all their colonies (see Illustration 11). Acceptance of the New Style (Gregorian) calendar was slower in Asia. It was adopted by Japan in 1873, by Egypt in 1875, by China in 1912, by Turkey in 1917 and by

---

THE NEW CALENDAR:
NON-CATHOLICS HOLD BACK

Non-Catholic countries did not wish to associate themselves with a calendar reformed under the direction of a Pope, even if it was more accurate. The conversion to the New Style/Gregorian calendar was indeed a gradual one as these figures show.

1582 – France, Italy, Luxembourg, Portugal, Spain
1584 – Belgium, Catholic German States, part of Netherlands
1587 – Hungary
1699–1700 – Denmark, Protestant Netherlands, Protestant German States
1752 – Britain and the American Colonies
1753 – Sweden
1812 – Switzerland, although a few Cantons changed in 1583
1867 – Alaska, after its purchase by the United States
1873 – Japan
1875 – Egypt
1912–1917 – Eastern Europe
1918 – Soviet Russia adopted the New Style/Gregorian calendar after the Russian Revolution. There followed a period of internal calendar reforms. The New Style/Gregorian calendar was not adopted again until 1940.
1923 – Greece

the U.S.S.R. in 1918. In 1923 Greece adopted it, becoming the last European country to do so. Both the United Kingdom and Japanese governments maintain the practice of dating government documents according to the year of their present monarch's reign despite adoption of the New Style (Gregorian) calendar for civil purposes.

The Julian calendar is still the official calendar used by many Eastern Orthodox Churches, such as the Orthodox Churches of Greece, Russia, Serbia and Romania. It is also the calendar used by scientists and historians for referring to dates prior to AD 1582. Christian holy days celebrated by both the eastern and western Churches do not fall upon the same day because of the time difference between the Julian and Gregorian calendars.

NETHERLANDS: THE EXCEPTION

All Christian countries except the Netherlands use the Roman/Gregorian names for the calendar months. In the Netherlands it is customary to use descriptive Dutch names. They are:

DUTCH NAME	ENGLISH
Lauwmaand	chilly month
Sprokelmaand	vegetation month
Lentmaand	spring month
Grasmaand	grass month
Blowmaand	flower month
Zomermaand	summer month
Hooymaand	hay month
Oostmaand	harvest month
Herstmaand	autumn month
Wynmaand	wine month
Slagtmaand	slaughter month
Wintermaand	winter month

THE DAY AND WEEK

The early Christians adopted the Roman custom of beginning a day at one minute after midnight. Each day was a 24-hour period measured from midnight to midnight including a period of darkness split by a period of light. The day's length was divided into two units of twelve equal hours by some countries and into 24 equal hours by others.

ILLUSTRATION 11. Old and New Style calendars. The American colonies were influenced by England's reluctance to adopt the Gregorian calendar. When they adopted the New Style calendar, dates were often followed by the letters O.S. (Old Style) to indicate they were based on the Julian calendar.

The custom of using a seven-day week as a measurement of time for keeping the Sabbath day was not legalized until AD 321 when it was declared law by the Christian Emperor Constantine.

No one is sure who decided how to name the days of the week. It is easy to observe the influence upon the very early Christians of the pagan names for the days. Table 8 illustrates this relationship between the ancient, pre-Christian and the Christian names for the days.

Today, the majority of Christians regard Sunday, the first day of the week, as their Sabbath Day to commemorate the resurrection of Jesus Christ on the third day after He was crucified. A minority of Christians recognize and celebrate Saturday as the Sabbath Day in strict adherence to Judaic law.

THE MONTH AND YEAR

When the old Roman calendar was reformed during the reign of Julius Caesar, the division of the year into twelve months was retained but the number of days assigned to some of the months changed. This was to help keep the year synchronized with the solar seasons. However, in doing so the months were no longer synchronized with the waxing and waning of the moon. The months as they were adopted by Christians are shown in Table 9.

The Julian calendar year is exactly 365.25 days long and the Gregorian calendar year 365.24 days long. Both calendars use the system of having regular years interspersed with leap years to help balance the lunar year with the solar year. Regular years have 365 days and leap years have 366 days.

TABLE 9
ORDER & LENGTH OF CHRISTIAN MONTHS

MONTH	LENGTH
January	31
February	28
March	31
April	30
May	31
June	30
July	31
August	31
September	30
October	31
November	30
December	31

FESTIVALS, HOLY DAYS & ANNIVERSARIES

Today the Christian Church is divided into several hundred sects. The customary ways that feasts, festivals and holy days are celebrated may vary between the many Christian sects and also from one country to another. The best example of this variety can be seen in the celebration of Christmas. The three main divisions of the Christian Church – Roman Catholic, Eastern Orthodox and Protestant – observe some festivals in common and some individually.

Advent

This is the first season of the church year, its starting date depending upon which day of the week Christmas may occur, but always including the four Sundays before Christmas Day. It is seen as a time of penitence and preparation for the celebration of Christ's birth.

Christmas/Feast of the Nativity (25 December)

This joyous holiday commemorates the birth of Jesus Christ. It is celebrated with a variety of special foods, drink, games, music, pageants, processions, yule fires, colorful lights, gift-giving and prayers. Although the customs may vary widely from country to country, the joy of the Christmas season is shared by all Christians. Research has led to questions about the accuracy of the date of 25 December as the true date of Jesus Christ's birth, with many scholars believing March or April to be more likely.

Solomon Grundy born on Monday
Christened on Tuesday
Married on Wednesday
Took ill on Thursday
Worse on Friday
Died on Saturday
Buried on Sunday
This is the end of Solomon Grundy.   (Trad.)

Feast of the Annunciation (25 March)

Some Christians commemorate the occasion of the appearance of an angel to Mary, the Mother of Jesus, telling her that she would give birth to a special child, the baby Jesus.

Shrove Tuesday/*Mardi Gras*

The date for this pre-Lenten festival is determined by the date of Easter Sunday. It occurs on the Tuesday preceding Ash Wednesday (see below). The festival is given to merrymaking with music, noisemakers, dancing, the spraying of friends with water, masquerades, parades and the eating of special foods. Early Christians served certain foods, such as pancakes, in order to use up the cooking fats and oils in the household because it was forbidden to eat fat or even to have it in the home during the period of Lent. The name *Mardi Gras* literally means 'Fat Tuesday' in French.

THE GREAT EASTER DEBATE

Early Christians disputed, sometimes quite bitterly, about the proper date for celebrating Easter. One side argued that since Jesus Christ died on a Passover Day, Easter should be celebrated on 14 Nisan, the same day Jews celebrate the Eve of Passover. The other side argued that since the resurrection of Jesus Christ took place on a Sunday, Easter should always be commemorated on a Sunday, pointing out that 14 Nisan could fall on any day of the week.

At the Council of Nicaea in AD 325, a majority of Christians decided that Easter should occur on a Sunday and never on the same day as Passover. A Metonic Cycle of nineteen years was adopted for setting the date for Easter. A particular year within the Metonic Cycle is referred to by a 'Golden Number' as shown above.

Gregorian Year	Metonic Cycle/ Golden Number	Easter Dates
1987	12	19 April
1988	13	03 April
1989	14	29 March
1990	15	15 April
1991	16	31 March
1992	17	19 April
1993	18	11 April
1994	19	03 April
1995	01	16 April
1996	02	07 April

Ash Wednesday

The date of Ash Wednesday is determined by the date of Easter Sunday. It occurs 40 days prior to Easter and is the first day of the Lenten period. Ash Wednesday is a solemn, holy day, usually devoted to prayer and worship. The name is derived from a custom practiced by some Christians of rubbing ashes on their foreheads on this day as a mark of sorrow for the sins they had committed during the preceding year.

Lent

The beginning date of Lent, a 40-day period of fasting and spiritual preparation prior to Easter, is determined by the occurrence of Easter Sunday. It commemorates the period of 40 days that Jesus Christ spent in retirement in the wilderness. Today, for some Christians, it is a period of fasting. However, the fast observed is not a total abstinence from food and drink but rather a self-imposed restriction on certain foods. At one time Lent meant a total abstinence from meats and fats, but through the centuries the dietary restrictions have been relaxed until now only a few devout Christians observe them. It is more customary for Christians to observe Lent by abstaining from amusements and devoting more time to prayer, the study of the scriptures and the performing of community service.

Palm Sunday

Palm Sunday occurs on the Sunday prior to Easter Sunday. It is a happy occasion recalling the triumphant entry of Jesus Christ into the city of Jerusalem, greeted by crowds waving palm branches, shortly before He was tried and crucified. Many churches are decorated with palm leaves, if they are available, or with branches from local trees.

Good Friday

Good Friday is the Friday prior to Easter Sunday. It is an especially solemn holy day, recalling the trial of Jesus Christ by Pontius Pilate, His sentence and His crucifixion. It is observed with prayer, worship, special music, and fasting by some Christians.

Easter/*Paschal* Feast

Easter can occur as early as 22 March or as late as 25 April. The first Christians differed on how to calculate the date for Easter. The Council of Nicaea in AD 325 ruled that Easter should occur on the first Sunday after the first full moon on or after the vernal equinox. In the early history of the Christian church, Easter was considered the most important Feast in the church year, an especially joyous festival because it celebrates the resurrection of Jesus Christ after His crucifixion. Today, the day is celebrated with hymns of praise and thanksgiving, processions, floral decorations, special foods and the wearing of new clothes.

Ascension Day

Ascension Day occurs 40 days after Easter Sunday, commemorating the bodily ascent of Jesus Christ into heaven after His resurrection. The day is sometimes referred to as Holy Thursday.

Whitsunday/Pentecost

Whitsunday is 50 days after Easter Sunday. It commemorates the appearance of the Holy Spirit of Christ to His followers after His resurrection and ascension. Some Christians used this day as a favorite time for baptism ceremonies, and as those being baptized dressed in white garments, it became known as White or Whit Sunday.

THE HIJRI CALENDAR – THE CALENDAR OF THE MUSLIMS

The Hijri calendar takes as its beginning a significant religious event – the great journey of the Prophet Muhammad and His companions from the city of Mecca to the city of Medina. The first year of the calendar is designated as 1 AH, the AH standing for *Anno Hejira*, which means the 'Year of the Emigration'. The year 1 AH coincides with the year AD 622.

Muhammad, the Prophet and Founder of Islam, united the diverse tribes of Arabia into a new civilization. Old pagan practices were cast aside and a new way of life based on His teachings was established. An individual's spiritual life was deemed to be so important that it took precedence over all other aspects of life. Devout Muslims, the followers of Islam, felt the need for a way to reckon time to help them obey the spiritual laws and disciplines decreed by Muhammad.

Praise be to God,
  Lord of the
  worlds!
The compassionate,
  the merciful . . .
Guide Thou us on
  the straight
  path . . .
  – Qur'án, 1:1–6

The sacred book of the Muslims, the Qur'án, established a calendar system that measured time by the natural rhythm of the moon. The adoption of a simple, lunar calendar was appropriate for the nomadic tribes of Arabia because their lives did not depend on the sun's cycle for the raising of crops. Under the guidance of 'Umar, the second caliph (the highest civil and religious leader), the regular use of an Islamic calendar was established around AD 634. At this time, the month of *Muharram* was made its first month even though Muhammad's journey from Mecca to Medina took place in the month of *Rabi'u'l-Avval*. The beginning and end of each month was also defined and the months were given names. No attempt was made to balance the year of twelve lunar months with the solar year.

The lunar year is approximately eleven days shorter than the solar year. Consequently, the beginning of a lunar calendar year slips back gradually through the solar seasons. The first day of the first month of the Hijri calendar occurs at the spring equinox only once in every $32^1/_2$ years. This results in an interesting phenomenon occurring every 33 years. On these occasions, Muslims can celebrate two new year's days in one Gregorian year. For example, 1 Muharram 1362 AH coincided with 8 January 1943 and 1 Muharram 1363 AH coincided with 28 December 1943.

THE DAY

For Muslims, a day begins at sunset and ends the following day at sunset. Each calendar day is a 24-hour period. None of the weekdays is designated as a day of rest corresponding to the Jewish *Shabbat* or the Christian Sabbath. Muslim legend suggests that it could not have been possible for God to have suffered fatigue after the creation of the world, therefore there is no need to observe a day of rest. However, *Al-Jum'ah* (Friday) is a special day because Muhammad first entered Medina on a Friday and also, according to Muslim belief, the Creation was finished on a Friday. Al-Jum'ah was established as the Day of Assembly (that is, of congregational prayer), by Muhammad

TABLE 10
DAYS OF THE HIJRI CALENDAR

ARABIC	ENGLISH	GREGORIAN EQUIVALENT
Al-Ahad	First Day	Sunday
Al-Ithnayn	Second Day	Monday
Ath-Thulathaa'	Third Day	Tuesday
Al-Arba'aa	Fourth Day	Wednesday
Al-Khamees	Fifth Day	Thursday
Al-Jum'ah	Day of Assembly	Friday
As-Sabt	Seventh Day	Saturday

Himself: "*O ye who believe! When the call is heard for prayer on the day of the assembly, haste unto remembrance of God, and leave your trading. That is better for you, if ye did but know*" (Qur'án, 62:9).

THE WEEK

The Hijri calendar adopted the Jewish and Christian tradition of grouping seven days together to form the unit of time we call a week. The names of the days of the week are given above.

THE MONTH

A month on the Hijri calendar begins about two days after the first appearance of the new moon when the crescent is first sighted. To solve the problem of a lunar month being $29\frac{1}{2}$ days long, the Hijri calendar alternates months of 29 or 30 days each. The month names of the old pagan Arabian calendar were adopted. Some of those months were named for the seasons but, when Muhammad adopted a strictly lunar calendar, the year fell out of phase with the seasons and the names of the months lost their former meaning. Table 11 gives the names, order and length of the months.

The month of *Safar* originally occurred in autumn at the time when leaves had turned yellow, hence its name derived from the word for that color. It was considered an unlucky month because, according to legend, it was during this month that Adam and Eve were expelled from the Garden of Eden. When first named, the months of *Jamadiyu'l-Avval* and *Jamadiyu'th-Thani* occurred in the winter season when rain had not fallen for some time and the ground was hard. Muhammad decreed that the months

ORDER	ARABIC	LENGTH
1	Muharram	30
2	Safar	29
3	Rabi'u'l-Avval	30
4	Rabi'u'th-Thani	29
5	Jamadiyu'l-Avval	30
6	Jamadiyu'th-Thani	29
7	Rajab	30
8	Sha'ban	29
9	Ramadan	30
10	Shavval	29
11	Dhi'l-Qa'dih	30
12	Dhi'l-Hijjih	29

TABLE 11

Months of THE HIJRI CALENDAR

of *Muharram, Rajab, Dhi'l-Qa'dih* and *Dhi'l-Hijjih* were sacred, forbidding Muslims to go to war or conduct raids during these months.

THE YEAR

The Hijri calendar is based on a 30-year cycle composed of 360 lunar months. It is a very accurate calendar and has been calculated to be only one day out every 2500 years of lunar-time reckoning. Common years have 354 days and leap years have 355 days. An intercalary day is added to Dhi'l-Hijjih, the twelfth month, in the second, fifth, seventh, tenth, thirteenth, sixteenth, eighteenth, 21st, 24th, 26th and 29th year of each 30-year cycle.

It is difficult to convert an exact Gregorian date to a Hijri one without the use of a table. Every 100 Gregorian years are approximately equal to 103 Hijri years. Every 100 Hijri years are approximately equal to 97 Gregorian years.

Users of the Gregorian calendar will not celebrate the turn of a century until the year 2000, but Muslims celebrated the turn of a century some years ago when they began their fifteenth century. According to the Gregorian calendar, that event occurred on 19 November 1979.

The Faith of Islam, as with Judaism and Christianity before it, has split into sects. Similarly, there are differences to be found among the various sects as to which significant occasions should be celebrated and how they should be celebrated, but the following are some of the main occasions recognized by the majority of Muslims.

FESTIVALS, HOLY DAYS AND ANNIVERSARIES

Al-Jum'ah (Friday Prayer)
Friday at noon has been designated as the time for

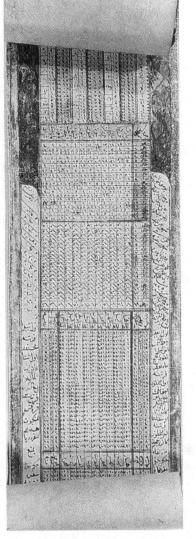

ILLUSTRATION 12. A nineteenth-century Hijri calendar.

congregational prayers to be observed by every male Muslim who is able to attend. Women are exempt from attending. The prayers are performed at the local mosque, or at some public gathering place if there is no mosque, and must be led by an Imam (priest). After the opening prayers are completed, the Imam delivers the *Khuthah* (sermon). He then reads passages from the Qur'án. To complete the prayer session, individuals may recite prayers of their choice in a low voice. Friday is also referred to by some Muslims as 'Adam's Birthday' to remind believers of the day when Adam was taken into Paradise.

Ras Al-Sana (New Year's Day, 1 Muharram)

The customs observed in celebrating the Muslim New Year vary from joyous feasting to solemn fasting. One of the traditions observed recalls the legend of the tree of life on the edge of Paradise. According to the legend, the tree bears one leaf for each human being in the world. On the eve of 1 Muharram an angel comes and shakes the tree vigorously causing many of the leaves to fall, and those whose names are on the fallen leaves are destined to die within the coming year. Muslims commemorate the occasion by offering prayers for the dead and by reading passages from the Qur'án that promise life after death. In some areas, Muslims dress in mourning clothes, erect black tents and decorate them with flowers and lighted lamps. Men, women and children gather in the streets to exchange greetings and wish each other good luck and protection from the angel of death. Some also exchange gifts of coins.

The Martyrdom of Husayn (10 Muharram)

On this date, Shi'ah Muslims honor the memory of the Imam Husayn, grandson of the Prophet Muhammad. Scenes from his life are re-enacted, concluding with a scene showing Husayn's death in battle. Sometimes a white horse and rider, painted with streaks of red or smeared with real blood, parade through the streets. Another custom is to give away dishes of sherbet in memory of Husayn's thirst on the battlefield. The commemoration of the martyrdom of Husayn, a sad and solemn occasion, is also a very emotional one and people freely express their grief over his loss.

'Ashura (10 Muharram)

Other Muslims celebrate a different, happier occasion on 10 Muharram. They recall the safe landing of Noah's Ark after the devastating flood. A legend relates the joy Noah experienced in surviving the flood and of being able to stand on solid ground once again. He asked his wife to make a pudding to celebrate the joyous occasion. Noah's wife gathered figs, raisins, dates and nuts and created a special, great pudding in honor of the occasion. Muslims who observe this tradition like to prepare and serve a similar special pudding on this day.

Ma'uled Al-Nabi (The Birthday of Muhammad, 11 Rabi'u'l-Avval)

The Prophet's birthday is the most joyful event celebrated during the Muslim year. The day begins with exploding firecrackers and booming cannons. In some Muslim countries fairs and processions are held. In other Muslim countries children are told wonderful tales of the birth and childhood of Muhammad. However, no matter in what way it is celebrated, the day is one for rejoicing. Mosques are decorated, verses of the Qur'án are recited, communities plan festivities and families prepare feasts. Since the actual date of Muhammad's birth is not known, some Muslims have adopted the custom of celebrating His birth on the same date as His death.

The Fast of *Ramadan* (1–30 Ramadan)

The entire ninth month is set aside as a special time of fasting. "*As to the month of Ramadan in which the Qur'án was sent down to be man's guidance, and an explanation of that guidance, and of that illumination, as soon as any one of you observeth the moon, let him set about the fast . . .*" (Qur'án 2:185). The name *Ramadan* is said to be derived from the Arabic word *ramz* which means 'to burn', presumably because the observance of the fast was intended to burn away sins. The goal of the fast for all dedicated Muslims is the development of greater self-discipline and self-control. During the fast, devout Muslims get up and eat their morning meal before sunrise. They refrain from both food and drink during the day and break their fast with an evening meal after the sun sets. The month of the fast is devoted to prayer, penance and strict obedience to the laws of Islam. Today, the date for the beginning of month of Ramadan is set by the Naval Observatory in Cairo, Egypt.

'Eedu-l-Fitr (The Festival of Fast Breaking, 1–3 Shavval)

There are two 'Eed festivals, which are the main Muslim feast days and each is a form of thanksgiving. 'Eedu-l-Fitr, sometimes referred to as 'The Small Feast', marks the end of the month-long fast of Ramadan. Muslims rejoice and express their gratitude to God for their individual achievements in service and their victories over human weaknesses. On the first day of the festival, Muslims express this thanksgiving by distributing alms to the poor and needy. The head of a family usually gives an amount equivalent to the cost of one meal for each member of his family. On the succeeding days, families put on new clothes and gather together for sumptuous feasts. Children are given candies, sweets and money to buy special treats and toys or necessities for school. It is also a time for friends to exchange gifts or cards and for great fairs to be held. Both of the joyful 'Eed festivals are celebrated for three days. Both 'Eed festivals are primarily religious occasions commemorated through public worship and the sharing of especially prepared foods with family and friends.

Hajj (Pilgrimage, 7 Dhi'l-Hijjih)

The Pilgrimage is a time in which individual Muslims, both male and female, seek spiritual renewal and enrichment. It is obligatory for every Muslim to make a Pilgrimage to Mecca at least once in his or her lifetime, if it is at all financially possible. During the ritual of Pilgrimage, all male pilgrims from kings to slaves become equals, as symbolized by the custom of dressing in two white sheets.

'Eedu-l-Adha (The Feast of Sacrifice, 10 Dhi'l-Hijjih)

The Feast of Sacrifice is the other 'Eed festival. It commemorates the historic event of Abraham's devotion when he was called upon to sacrifice his son Ishmael. Abraham demonstrated his complete obedience to God by his willingness to perform that act, although it was not carried out (see Genesis 22:15, where according to Jewish tradition it was his son Isaac, not Ishmael, that Abraham was prepared to sacrifice). Today, animals such as sheep, goats and camels are ritually sacrificed and then the meat is distributed to the poor and needy.

THE BADÍ' CALENDAR – THE CALENDAR OF THE BAHÁ'ÍS

The loftiest station which human perception can soar and the utmost height which the minds and souls of man can scale are but signs created through the potency of Thy command and tokens manifested through the power of Thy Revelation.

– The Báb

The Bahá'í Era (BE) begins in the year when the Báb (the 'Gate'), the Martyr-Herald of the Bahá'í Faith, declared that He was the forerunner of a new Manifestation of God who would soon appear. The Báb made His declaration in Persia on the eve of 5 Jamadiyu'l-Avval 1260 AH according to the Muslim calendar, or 23 May 1844 according to the Christian calendar. One of the ways He signaled to the world the importance of His mission was by inaugurating a new calendar, which Bahá'ís know as the Badí' (new, wonderful) calendar. This calendar abandons the lunar year of the Muslims and adopts a solar-based system.

THE DAY
For Bahá'ís the day begins at sunset as it does for Jews and Muslims. It would seem that the use of a natural phenomenon for measuring the day has continuous appeal. The nineteen days in a Bahá'í

	TABLE 12	
DAYS OF THE BADÍʿ CALENDAR		
ARABIC	ENGLISH	GREGORIAN EQUIVALENT
Jalál	Glory	Saturday
Jamál	Beauty	Sunday
Kamál	Perfection	Monday
Fidál	Grace	Tuesday
ʿIdál	Justice	Wednesday
Istijlál	Majesty	Thursday
Istiqlál	Independence	Friday

month have been named after some of the attributes of God and are the same as the names given to the nineteen months. For example, the first day of each month is named *Bahá* (Splendor), the second day is named *Jalál* (Glory), the third day is named *Jamál* (Beauty) and so forth (see Table 13).

THE WEEK

In the Badíʿ calendar, there is very little emphasis on any group of days smaller than the nineteen-day month. However, for those who wish, the year has also been divided into 52 weeks. As with the months, the seven days of the week are named after attributes of God. The day names and order appear in Table 12.

Each date may be identified by three names, those of the month, the day of the month and the day of the week. No special religious significance is given to any of the days of the week that would correspond to the Jewish *Shabbat*, the Christian Sabbath or the Muslim Al-Jumʿah.

THE MONTH

There are nineteen months of nineteen days each. The nineteen months have also been named after attributes of God.

The first day of the Bahá'í year.

Month of Bahá — Mar. 21, 22, 23, 24, 25, 26, 27, 28, 29, 30, 31, April 1, 2, 3, 4, 5, 6, 7, 8

Month of Jalál — 9, 10, 11, 12, 13, 14, 15, 16, 17, 18, 19, 20, 21, 22, 23, 24, 25, 26, 27
- 13 The anniversary of the Declaration of Bahá'u'lláh / The first day of Ridván

Month of Jamál — 28, 29, 30, May 1, 2, 3, 4, 5, 6, 7, 8, 9, 10, 11, 12, 13, 14, 15, 16
- 2 The ninth day of Ridván
- 5 The twelfth day of Ridván

Month of 'Azamat — 17, 18, 19, 20, 21, 22, 23, 24, 25, 26, 27, 28, 29, 30, 31, June 1, 2, 3, 4
- 7 The anniversary of the declaration of the Báb
- 13 The anniversary of the ascension of Bahá'u'lláh

Month of Núr — 5, 6, 7, 8, 9, 10, 11, 12, 13, 14, 15, 16, 17, 18, 19, 20, 21, 22, 23

Month of Rahmat — 24, 25, 26, 27, 28, 29, 30, July 1, 2, 3, 4, 5, 6, 7, 8, 9, 10, 11, 12
- 16 The anniversary of the martyrdom of the Báb

Month of Kalimát — 13, 14, 15, 16, 17, 18, 19, 20, 21, 22, 23, 24, 25, 26, 27, 28, 29, 30, 31

Month of Kamál — Aug. 1, 2, 3, 4, 5, 6, 7, 8, 9, 10, 11, 12, 13, 14, 15, 16, 17, 18, 19

Month of Asmá' — 20, 21, 22, 23, 24, 25, 26, 27, 28, 29, 30, 31, Sept. 1, 2, 3, 4, 5, 6, 7

Month of Izzat — 8, 9, 10, 11, 12, 13, 14, 15, 16, 17, 18, 19, 20, 21, 22, 23, 24, 25, 26

Month of Mashíyyat — 27, 28, 29, 30, Oct. 1, 2, 3, 4, 5, 6, 7, 8, 9, 10, 11, 12, 13, 14, 15

Month of 'Ilm — 16, 17, 18, 19, 20, 21, 22, 23, 24, 25, 26, 27, 28, 29, 30, 31, Nov. 1, 2, 3
- 5 The anniversary of the birth of the Báb

Month of Qudrat — 4, 5, 6, 7, 8, 9, 10, 11, 12, 13, 14, 15, 16, 17, 18, 19, 20, 21, 22
- 9 The anniversary of the birth of Bahá'u'lláh

Month of Qawl — 23, 24, 25, 26, 27, 28, 29, 30, Dec. 2, 3, 4, 5, 6, 8, 9, 10, 11
- 4 The Day of the Covenant
- 6 The Ascension of 'Abdu'l-Bahá

Month of Masá'il — 12, 13, 14, 15, 16, 17, 18, 19, 20, 21, 22, 23, 25, 26, 27, 28, 29, 30

	Month of Sharaf	31		Month of ‘Alá’	2
2		Jan. 1	1	The first day of the Bahá'í Fast	
3		2			
4		3	2		3
5		4	3		4
6		5	4		5
7		6	5		6
8		7	6		7
9		8	7		8
		9	8		9
1		10	9		10
2		11	10		11
3		12	11		12
4		13	12		13
5		14	13		14
6		15	14		15
7		16	15		16
8		17	16		17
9		18	17		18
1	Month of Sultán	19	18		19
2		20	19	The last day of the Bahá'í Fast	20
3		21			
4		22			
5		23			
6		24			
7		25			
8		26			
9		27			
		28			
1		29			
2		30			
3		31			
4		Feb. 1			
5		2			
6		3			
7		4			
8		5			
9		6			
1	Month of Mulk	7			
2		8			
3		9			
4		10			
5		11			
6		12			
7		13			
8		14			
9		15			
		16			
1		17			
2		18			
3		19			
4		20			
5		21			
6		22			
7		23			
8		24			
9		25			
	Intercalary Days	26			
		27			
		28/9			
		Mar. 1			

ILLUSTRATION 13. A design for the Badí‘ calendar used by Bahá'ís, showing corresponding Gregorian calendar dates.

TABLE 13

Months of the Badí‘ Calendar

ARABIC	ENGLISH
1. *Bahá*	Splendor
2. *Jalál*	Glory
3. *Jamál*	Beauty
4. *‘Azamat*	Grandeur
5. *Núr*	Light
6. *Rahmat*	Mercy
7. *Kalimát*	Words
8. *Kamál*	Perfection
9. *Asmá’*	Names
10. *‘Izzat*	Might
11. *Mashíyyat*	Will
12. *‘Ilm*	Knowledge
13. *Qudrat*	Power
14. *Qawl*	Speech
15. *Masá’il*	Questions
16. *Sharaf*	Honor
17. *Sultán*	Sovereignty
18. *Mulk*	Dominion
19. *‘Alá’*	Loftiness

The first day of each month is designated a Feast Day. Bahá'ís observe this occasion by gathering together for prayers and readings from the writings of the three central figures of the Bahá'í Faith, the Báb, Bahá'u'lláh and ‘Abdu'l-Bahá; for consultation on the affairs of the community; and for socializing and refreshments. The Feast Day is the center of Bahá'í spiritual and community life much as *Shabbat* is the center of Jewish life.

THE YEAR

The Badí' calendar is based on a solar year of 365 days, five hours, 48 minutes and 46 seconds. As the year is divided into nineteen months of nineteen days each, a quick calculation will suffice to show that this only equals 361 days. To balance the calendar year with the solar year, four days are added in common years and five days in leap years. Leap years occur once every four years unless it is necessary to adjust the beginning of a year so that it will coincide with the vernal equinox.

The first day of the Bahá'í year is astronomically fixed. Like the ancient Persian calendar and the modern Iranian one, the first day of the year of the Badí' calendar coincides with the vernal equinox. If the vernal equinox precedes the setting of the sun, New Year's Day is celebrated on that calendar day. If the vernal equinox occurs after the setting of the sun, New Year's Day is celebrated on the following calendar day. The Badí' calendar year commences on the first day of the month of *Bahá* (Splendor). By Gregorian reckoning, that day falls on 21 March. It can, although rarely, fall on 22 March if the vernal equinox occurs after the setting of the sun.

The Báb grouped the years into cycles of nineteen years. Each nineteen-year cycle is called a '*Vahíd*'. The name *Vahíd* signifies the unity of God. Nineteen cycles grouped together make up a period entitled '*Kull-i-Shay*'. This translates literally as 'all things' and refers to the creative power of God to make all things new.

When the Báb inaugurated His new calendar, He made it conditional upon the sanction of the Manifestation of God who was to follow Him. Bahá'u'lláh, whom Bahá'ís recognize as that promised manifestation, endorsed the Báb's calendar, making only the minor adjustment of establishing when the intercalary days should occur. He named the intercalary days '*Ayyam-i-Há*' (Days of Há) and declared that they should immediately precede 'Alá', the nineteenth month.

FESTIVALS, HOLY DAYS AND ANNIVERSARIES

Naw-Rúz (New Year, 21 March)

Naw-Rúz is a feast of rejoicing and hospitality that celebrates a spiritual springtime along with nature's springtime (in the northern hemisphere). To celebrate this joyous occasion, families and friends may gather together to recite prayers and read from the Holy Books, then enjoy fellowship, music and/or dancing, and share refreshments. There are no prescribed or traditional ways of observing Naw-Rúz and each community is free to plan its celebration as it wishes.

The Festival of Ridván (21 April to 2 May)

This twelve-day period is considered the most important and holiest observance in the Bahá'í year. The Festival of Ridván commemorates the last twelve days that Bahá'u'lláh, His family and His companions spent at a garden estate near Baghdád prior to Bahá'u'lláh's further exile. It was during this period that Bahá'u'lláh made His first public declaration of His mission. The significance and joy of the occasion to the followers of Bahá'u'lláh is reflected in the name given to that site after His declaration: the 'Garden of Ridván', meaning the Garden of Paradise. The first, ninth and twelfth days of Ridván are celebrated as special holy days and there is a recognition of spiritual renewal among the Bahá'ís during this festive time. Bahá'ís also hold their annual election to their administrative bodies during the Ridván period.

Declaration of the Báb (23 May)

The Declaration of the Báb is a joyous event for Bahá'ís who commemorate the time when the Báb declared that He was both the Promised Qá'im whose return was anticipated by Muslims and 'the Gate' through which a new Manifestation of God would soon appear to mankind. Bahá'ís like to gather together on this anniversary to recite prayers, to read selected passages from the Bahá'í writings, and for fellowship.

Ascension of Bahá'u'lláh (29 May)

This holy day recalls the passing of Bahá'u'lláh on 13 'Azamat 49 BE (29 May 1892). Bahá'ís meet to read prayers at the same hour of the day that Bahá'u'lláh passed away.

Martyrdom of the Báb (9 July)

The public execution of the Báb by firing squad in the barracks square in the city of Tabríz, Iran on this day in 1850 is commemorated on this solemn anniversary.

Birth of the Báb (20 October)

The Báb was born on 1 Muharram, 1235 AH (20 October 1819). The anniversary of His birth is a happy occasion when Bahá'í families and their friends come together for devotional readings, feasting and fellowship.

Birth of Bahá'u'lláh (12 November)

Bahá'u'lláh was born on 2 Muharram 1233 AH (12 November 1817). This joyous occasion for Bahá'ís is celebrated by the holding of public meetings or by private gatherings to recall the life of Bahá'u'lláh.

On all of the above Holy Days, Bahá'ís refrain from working at their trade or profession, and Bahá'í students do not attend school or college.

Day of the Covenant (26 November)

This day set aside to honor 'Abdu'l-Bahá, the eldest son of Bahá'u'lláh whom He instructed Bahá'ís to follow as His successor upon His death. 'Abdu'l-Bahá is also especially revered for being the perfect exemplar of His father's teachings, and the only interpreter of His father's revelation. Bahá'ís hold gatherings on this anniversary and invite their friends to help them celebrate the uniqueness of 'Abdu'l-Bahá's station.

Ascension of 'Abdu'l-Bahá (28 November)

The Ascension of 'Abdu'l-Bahá is a solemn anniversary marking the death of 'Abdu'l-Bahá. It is usually observed with the reading of prayers at the same hour of the day on which His death occurred in 1921.

Ayyám-i-Há (Intercalary Days)

The Intercalary Days occur after the end of the eighteenth month and before the beginning of the nineteenth month. There are four intercalary days in common years and five in leap years. On the Gregorian calendar, the days fall upon 26, 27, and 28 February and 1 March, and are devoted to hospitality, charitable acts and service to the community. Some Bahá'ís exchange gifts with their family and friends at this time. The Intercalary Days are also a time when Bahá'ís prepare themselves for the approaching Fast.

The Fast
The month of 'Alá' (2 to 20 March) is a period of fasting that is observed annually at the close of the calendar year. Complete abstinence from food and drink is observed between the hours of sunrise and sunset. Believers are free to eat a meal prior to sunrise and again after the sun sets. This period of fasting is adhered to by Bahá'ís between the ages of fifteen and 70 except for the "*traveler, the ailing, those who are with child or giving suck* . . ."

The Fast occurs at the time of year when the hours of daylight and darkness are about equal throughout the world and at a time when there are fewer extremes in climatic conditions in temperate regions. It is not intended to be a physical hardship, but rather to be a time for spiritual growth and renewal, much as the period of Lent is for Christians and the month of Ramadan for Muslims.

CHAPTER

WAYS OF CELEBRATING AROUND THE WORLD

Here are set our
hand-drums
and drums . . .
The large bells
and drums fill
the ear;
The various
dances are
grandly
performed.
– Ancient
Chinese
Scriptures

It is now obvious that people of many different religions were united in feeling a need to rejoice and to know when to rejoice. Another point of unity can be seen in the similar ways in which people of widely diverse cultures and geographical locations choose to celebrate the sacred events of their calendar year.

Independently, people around the world developed common ways of celebrating festivals, feasts and holy days. Sometimes they used specific practices in a slightly different way, or for slightly different reasons, yet the similarity is there. Since ancient times, a number of recurring elements have been used by most of the world's cultures in observing various religious events. Here are some well-known examples out of the hundreds of expressions of rejoicing around the globe.

LIGHT
Candles, lamps and lanterns have been part of

religious rites and ceremonies for thousands of years. In Hinduism, it is an ancient custom to celebrate the annual festival called *Diwali* by lighting many lamps, which are then placed on rooftops and around the thresholds of homes. Diwali, a happy holiday, is known as the 'Festival of Lights'.

In various oriental cultures, artisans construct colorful lanterns of paper, place burning candles inside them and then string them up to make special occasions more festive. Many generations of Jews have made an annual pilgrimage to the Tomb of Rabbi Shimon in the Holy Land to cover his tomb with lighted candles in his honor and dance in front of the tomb.

Some Christians light candles as votive offerings to saints. This can be done for a variety of reasons such as to seek a speedy recovery from sickness, or to request safety and protection, or to ask for a blessing either for oneself or a loved one. A burning candle in other sacred Christian ceremonies symbolizes the power of God or godly attributes such as truth and purity. In certain Christian processions, a flaming candle may symbolize the light of God or an individual's joy in his own belief.

There are also occasions when the use of lights may be for a sorrowful reason, such as in the mourning rites for the death of a loved one. In Buddhism, lighted lanterns feature as part of the ceremony called the 'Festival of the Dead'.

DANCE

Dance was, and still is, an instinctive way of expressing feelings of joy or sorrow in many cultures. It was quite natural, therefore, to include dance as a part of worship or prayer. Early dance involved the use of the whole body, especially the hands. It is believed by many that the combined physical and spiritual excitement produced in dance led to the ecstasy experienced by dervishes, shamans, oracles, and visionaries.

In ancient agricultural societies, dances were performed in springtime in the belief that they would stimulate the growth of the crops. For example, high leaping dances were believed to inspire and stimulate growth of tall crops. The Morris dances of England were

ILLUSTRATION 14. Procession and lanterns in Malaysia. On the fifteenth day of the New Year's celebration (*Yuan Tan*) there is the Lantern Festival, when children parade with lighted lanterns and the mythical dragon. The lanterns symbolize torches used to help people find the heavenly spirits who fly in the light of the first full moon.

first performed in the spring to wake up the earth after it had slept all winter and to prepare it for receiving the seed.

Early Christian bishops led believers in sacred dances in the churches and in front of the tombs of martyrs but in AD 692 the practice was forbidden. In spite of this, sacred dance continued in some French provinces on saints' days as late as the eighteenth century.

DECORATIONS

Special days not only needed to be noted on a calendar but they also needed some visual signs to remind believers of their occurrence and their importance. Before the days of shopping centers and technology, people looked to nature to provide materials for decorating their homes and holy places. The purpose of the decorations was to provide visible symbols for the faithful to remind them which sacred occasion was being celebrated and to help create a suitable atmosphere for the occasion. What nature had to offer depended upon geographical location and the season of the year.

In most places nature provided tree branches. People in many cultures have used branches from evergreen trees, blossoming trees, broad leaf trees and palm trees. Sometimes they tie fruit, flowers, berries or nuts to the branches to make them look more festive. Where trees were not plentiful, boughs from smaller shrubs were often used. Bundles of cut grain such as wheat, barley, rice and corn were tied together for decorating at harvest times. Clusters of corn ears, gourds and other vegetables might also be used for added color.

During early spring festivals, before there is much greenery available for decorating, it is the custom in some cultures to plant seeds indoors in small bowls. The sprouting seeds would provide a bit of green in honor of the occasion. Nature has also bountifully provided fragrant herbs and spices for use as decorating materials, with the pleasant odors and sweet smells intensifying the enjoyment of holiday festivities.

Nature is not the only source of decorating materials. Banners, flags, streamers, and fantastic shapes have traditionally been made from paper, cloth and wood, the designs limited only by the imagination of the artisans who created them.

Lights also play an important part in decorating. People throughout the world have used oil lamps, candles, and beautiful paper lanterns to add sparkle to their festivities. Today, it is more likely to be electric or battery-powered lights providing a safe method of brightening up a holiday.

FASTING

Most religions set aside some special time during the year for fasting. Methods of fasting vary from total abstinence from food and drink to simply abstaining from certain foods at certain times. The reasons for fasting are as variable as the methods. To some, it is a means of penance or accounting for personal sin, while to others it is a spiritual preparation before making a sacrifice or performing a sacred ritual. It can be an integral part of the mourning process after the death of a saint or prophet, or a means of purification. In some cultures, fasting is used as a spur to spiritual growth.

FIRE

Ritual fires, bonfires and perpetual flames have been used through the ages as symbols of purification, as a power to expel or bar the approach of evil, and as a symbol of eternal faith. The Zoroastrian Parsis are a well-known example of people who still include the use of fire in their religious ceremonies. Parsis do not worship fire, but view it as the earthly symbol of divine, infinite and heavenly light. To them fire is the great purifier. Semitic, Greek and Australian peoples have also used fire as a symbol of purification. The use of a perpetual flame or fire at holy sites to honor a divine power has been practiced over the centuries and continues to the present mainly through the use of eternal flames at monuments honoring national heroes or those who died in war.

Bonfires once played an important part in some religious celebrations. Small fires would be lit and the celebrants would dance and sing around them. A few brave souls would jump over the fires in the

ILLUSTRATION 15. Dance and Drums in Morocco. With a *bendir* drum providing the rhythm, these Berbers produce a magnificent spectacle.

hope it would bring them good luck. Even the burning of a yule log in the hearth on Christmas Eve is a survival of a pagan custom practiced in early England, the original meaning of which has been lost in history.

In some cultures, fire-wheels were constructed by tying straw to wooden wheels, setting them on fire and rolling them down hillsides. Fire-wheels symbolized the sun and their use was a springtime ritual to insure fertile fields and protect against natural disasters. This custom can still be witnessed as part of some Easter celebrations.

April

SUNDAY	MONDAY	TUESDAY	WEDNESDA
Easter –Christian Palm Sunday – Eastern Orthodox Nisfu Sha'ban – Islamic 3	Nat. Holiday – Hungary, Senegal Easter Monday – Christian 4	Ch'ing Ming Festival – Chinese 5	Chakri Day – Thailand Organization of the Churc Mormon Festival of the Sardine – S (date approx.) 6
Pascha (Easter) – Eastern Orthodox 10	Sham-el-Neseem – Egypt, Sudan 11	 12	Baisakhi – Bangladesh, H Sikh Songkran, Thingyan (Solar Year) – Asia 13
Nat. Holiday – Democratic Kampuchea, Syrian Arab Republic Sechseläuten – Switzerland (through 4-18) 17	Nat. Holiday – Zimbabwe Ramadan begins – Islamic 18	Nat. Holiday – Sierra Leone 19	 20
 24	Anzac Day – Australia, New Zealand 25	Nat. Holiday – United Rep. of Tanzania 26	Nat. Holiday – Afghanista Togo 27

THURSDAY	FRIDAY	SATURDAY
	April Fool's Day Good Friday – Christian **1**	International Children's Book Day Pesach (Passover) – Jewish (through 4-9) **2**
World Health Day Women's Day – Mozambique **7**	Buddha's Birthday – Japan Good Friday – Eastern Orthodox **8**	**9**
Pan American Day Nawabarsha (New York) – India, Nepal Water-Sprinkling Festival (New Year) – Dai (China) (date approx.) **14**	**15**	Nat. Holiday – Denmark **16**
Nat. Holiday – Israel Feast of Ridván – Bahá'í (through 5-2) Kartini Day – Indonesia **21**	**22**	St. George's Day – Christian Children's Day – Turkey **23**
28	Nat. Holiday – Japan Arbor Day – U.S.A. Adargan Jashan (Fire Festival) – Parsi **29**	Nat. Holiday – Netherlands Walpurgis Night – Northern Europe Weesakha Puja, Buddha Purnima. Wesak (Buddha's Birthday) – Buddhist **30**

ILLUSTRATION 16.
A page from a UNICEF wall calendar, showing an international view with religious and national holidays from around the world on a Gregorian calendar.

ILLUSTRATION 17. Fire Festival in Japan. Giant pine torches are carried up steps along the mountainside in front of the Kumano-Nachi Shrine. This fire purification rite is an old and integral part of Shinto-Buddhism.

In ancient times the ashes from the yule logs, bonfires and fire-wheels were thought to have magic powers and were saved to spread over the fields to insure good crops and a successful harvest. Other cultures used fire first to expel the decadent old life and then to rekindle new spiritual life.

FOOD AND DRINK

Joyous occasions can be made more joyous when food and drink are a part of the celebration. Sometimes food can be part of solemn occasions. Frequently, the kinds of food eaten at a holiday or festive occasion are symbolic and form a part of the commemoration. For example, in the Jewish *Seder* Feast at Passover, specific foods are eaten to remind Jews of the history and suffering of their ancestors. The well-known Easter egg may be served by Christians at Easter to symbolize Christ's tomb. Roast duck baked with a special red marinade may be served at Chinese New Year to symbolize good luck. Sweets like a special pudding may be served at the Muslim holiday 'Ashura to recall Noah's joy when he walked on dry land again after the great flood.

The importance of food in the lives of our ancestors was reflected in both positive and negative ways. Some foods were prohibited for spiritual reasons while others were specially served as a part of worship itself. The best known of these sacred foods is the Holy Eucharist (Communion), when bread and wine are partaken of by some Christians in a ritual performed to remember the body and blood of Jesus Christ.

JOYFUL NOISE

Gongs, bells, drums, cymbals, rattles, horns and other instruments and noise-makers are used in a wide variety of ways as part of religious celebrations. Throughout time, sound has been used to awaken spring, to celebrate the harvest, to mourn the dead, to frighten away evil spirits, to attract the attention of a deity when offering praise and thanksgiving or as a charm against evil spirits.

Gongs and Bells

In ancient times bells were tied to animals and people to protect the wearers from evil spirits. Even today, bells are often tied to the necks of cows, goats and camels for this reason. Bells in church towers, now used to call the faithful to prayer, were once used to drive away the evil spirits before the faithful came to pray. In the Middle Ages, hand-bells were used at funerals to call the faithful to pray on behalf of the departed one. Before the time of Christ, bells in the temples of the East called the souls of the departed to the funeral feast that had been prepared for them. Both Hindus and Buddhists use bells or gongs to attract the attention of the deity and to summon the deity to the offered ceremonies or prayers. Bells were also used in Buddhist temples as a part of the purification ritual. Early Jews also used bells as well as the ram's horn (*shofar*) and in the Book of Exodus (28:33) mention is made of bells being used on the priestly garments of Aaron.

Drums

In some societies drums have been used to produce a feeling of great excitement during religious ceremonies, invoking religious fervor and joy at festivals, processions, and ceremonies ranging from sacrifices to weddings. Drums have also been used to drive away danger and evil spirits.

Biblical references give evidence that drums have been connected with religion for at least 5000 years. This has been confirmed by archaeological excavations. There are many types of drums, a fact that gives strong support to the theory that the drum is a universal instrument. Even a newly invented percussion instrument such as the modern steel drum was first developed in Trinidad to add joy to noisy festivities at the pre-Lenten Carnival celebrations.

Music

The human voice is the most universal of all instruments. Psalms, hymns, carols, chants and other sacred songs have been written for special religious occasions to express praise, hope, thanksgiving, joy, sadness and mercy. Musical expression has been used to heighten religious feeling and to produce a state of exhilaration, sometimes called emotional intoxication. The human voice is often joined by other instruments to make music that expresses reverence, praise and spiritual joy.

ILLUSTRATION 18. Food in Portugal. These offering trays, made up of 30 special bread rolls surrounded by symbols of the Holy Spirit, are carried in a procession culminating at the entrance of the town's main church where they are blessed. On the following day the *peza* (blessed bread), together with meat and wine, are distributed to the poor.

PAGEANTS AND PROCESSIONS

It is believed that processions may have grown out of the ancient pagan custom of acting out the death and resurrection of the seasons. Religious processions have also been used to exhibit sacred objects so that their potency and blessing can be shed over more believers, while other processions honor saints or seek their protection.

A pageant is a play that serves to recall events in religious history and is usually staged in a particular location. There are, however, some very elaborate processions that include scenes staged on moving platforms.

PILGRIMAGE

The practice of pilgrimage has been described as a prolonged procession. From ancient times it has been the custom for believers to make journeys to sites holy to their faith, to renew religious vows, to offer penance for wrongdoing, to worship and, sometimes, to seek good fortune. Pilgrimage has been, and still is, practiced by Hindus, Jews, Zoroastrians, Buddhists, Christians, Sikhs, Muslims and Bahá'ís.

PRAYER

All of the world's great religions have taught the necessity of prayer. People offer prayers as a means of seeking protection, forgiveness, health, help or as a way to give thanks. The practice of prayer varies greatly between religions and cultures. Prayers may be offered in private or public places. They may be offered by a religious official, public figure, head of a family, or by any individual. But, wherever or by whomever the prayers are offered, it is universally accepted that pure, sincere intentions must be present. Prayer, as a means of communicating with a supreme being, is seen as an expression of faith and a means of spiritual growth.

SACRIFICE

The meaning of sacrifice or what constitutes a sacrifice has changed over the centuries. At one time in the history of mankind, it meant that humans were ritually killed to appease or please a god. At other times, sacrifice meant the ritual killing of small animals to insure good crops, to seek divine forgiveness for wrongdoing, or to ask for divine favors. The need to offer sacrifice seems to have originated in an overwhelming sense of sin and the need to atone for that sin, or a profound need for assistance from a supernatural power.

A more modern view of sacrifice is one in which a believer offers something of value to a supreme being. That person might offer time, energy, talent, possessions or money as a gift to his/her religion or community. Whatever the occasion, the amount given is not what is important, but rather the deprivation the person undergoes to offer the gift and the sincerity behind the sacrifice.

WATER

Water is the most common element used around the world to symbolize spiritual purification. The desire for purification after contact with a person perceived to be unclean (either diseased or sinful) is widespread. In some traditions, ceremonial bathing occurs before the offer of a sacrifice, before kindling a sacred fire or before beginning to pray or worship.

Other modern practices using water in sacred ceremonies of purification include the rites of baptism, the ceremonial washing of the dead before burial, the use of holy water and the use of water as a rain-charm.

Sprinkling or splashing young women with water to insure their fertility is an ancient custom that has lost its meaning but is perpetuated by Christians in Europe and South America at pre-Lenten Carnival time. Carnival celebrants take great delight in throwing colored or perfumed water on passers-by or by splashing them with water from water pistols. In Bolivia, enterprising boys and girls fill blown eggs with water and throw them at each other.

Other cultures enjoy splashing friends too. Hindu children celebrate Holi, a festival that welcomes the coming of spring, by dousing their friends with crimson and saffron-colored water. They use pans, pitchers, water pistols and bamboo blowpipes to carry the water and shower each other amidst squeals and laughter. Buddhist children in Burma celebrate their New Year with a water festival. While the children are busy spraying each other with water, their parents pour jars of water on the ground and recite prayers to welcome the New Year.

Feet-washing

The ceremonial washing of feet was practiced by early Jews, who believed it to be necessary to wash away the dirt of the road before one could be worthy to worship God. Early Christians also practiced ritual feet-washing and hand-washing before entering a church to worship. Today, during the observance of the Holy Week prior to Easter, Eastern Orthodox, Roman Catholic, and some Protestant Christians re-enact the drama of Jesus Christ washing the feet of the twelve Apostles before the Passover celebrations. Every devout Muslim not only washes his feet before reciting daily prayers but also ritually washes his hands, lower arms and face.

UNITY
IN DIVERSITY:
AN
OVERVIEW

UNIVERSAL PROBLEMS & CREATIVE SOLUTIONS

We have all inherited the collective wisdom of our forebears, including the results of their desire to measure and record time. Not all, but a select few of our ancient ancestors spent a lifetime observing the course of the sun, the movement of stars and constellations, and the waxing and waning of the moon. These sky-watchers, usually priests or early astronomers, had an amazing perseverance in faithfully observing the movement of the stars, the sun and the moon, day after day and year after year. And there were no 'Skywatcher of the Year' awards to acknowledge their skills. The priest-astronomers did, however, have a power and influence in their communities that must have been a reward in itself. As they watched the movement of the stars and the course of the sun, the venerable skywatchers gave their imagina-

Consider the sun. Were it to say now, "I am the sun of yesterday," it would speak the truth. And should it, bearing the sequence of time in mind, claim to be other than that sun, it still would speak the truth.

– Bahá'u'lláh

tions free rein. In the daytime, they would follow the course of the sun on the horizon and give names to the configurations they saw along the path, while during the long nights they imagined that some of the groups of stars resembled the shapes of mythical animals and people. They not only gave the stars names, but they also invented stories and developed wonderful legends about them. One of the best-known groups of stars in the northern hemisphere is Ursa Major, which means the Great Bear. In Greek mythology, Zeus changed the lovely Callisto into a bear to protect her from his jealous wife. Callisto's son, not knowing the bear was his mother, tried to kill it. Then Zeus changed him into a little bear (Ursa Minor) and pulled them both into the sky to save them from harm, stretching their tails as he did so. Today we also know Ursa Major by many different popular names such as the Big Dipper, the Big Wagon and the Plough.

So enamored are we of the printed word and modern technology that we find it difficult to recognize that some primitive civilizations possessed great skills even without a written language to record them, or modern technology to carry out their plans. Who could possibly say that the people who were able to construct the megaliths in England at Stonehenge, the pyramids in Egypt, the great terracotta army in China and the solar observatory tower at Hovenweep, were not intelligent, skillful and creative? It also took real understanding to foretell the spring and autumn equinoxes and the winter and summer solstices. In agricultural societies this was not a clever trick, but rather an imperative for survival. To be able to accurately forecast the time to plant and when to harvest could mean the difference between a bumper or a poor crop, and therefore the difference between survival until the next growing season and death. Life was harsh, yet our ancestors still managed to celebrate joyously the seasons and holy festivals that punctuated their precarious existence.

THE DESIRE TO WORSHIP

Along with timekeeping systems, we have also inherited a marvelous spiritual history from our ancestors. Although our forebears interpreted the nature of a supernatural power in a variety of ways and developed different methods of devotion and reverence, they were united in feeling a need to worship. Awed by the phenomena of nature and creation, they made an attempt to praise, and sometimes to appease, a power greater than themselves. Many scholars believe it was this deep desire to worship that inspired the development of ways to measure time, to organize it into convenient units and to record and forecast dates.

COMMON WAYS OF CELEBRATING

Strange as it may seem, our ancestors developed similar ways of expressing their reverential joy and sorrow. For example, candles are used by Hindus to celebrate the festival Diwali, by Jews at Chanukah, by Buddhists at Obon, by some Christians at Christmas and by Muslims on Muhammad's Birthday. Hindus enjoy dancing and joyful noise on the festival of Holi, Jews at Simchath Torah, Christians at Mardi Gras, Buddhists at Esala Perahera, and Muslims at 'Eedu-l-Fitr. Pageants, processions and use of water are also an integral part of the celebrations of many faiths. So, although the differences in calendar systems have long been associated with the ways groups identify and distinguish themselves from the others around them, in reality the expressions of joy and sorrow, of ecstasy and devotion, have much in common.

THE INTERNATIONAL DATELINE

The International Dateline is an imaginary line drawn through the middle of the Pacific Ocean, from north to south. It marks the place where each new calendar day begins. It generally follows the 180th meridian but the dateline bends a little in places to avoid the problem of having two different calendar dates for the same day in one country. If the dateline split a country, on the west side of the dateline it would be a Monday, while on the east side the day would be a Sunday.

A GLOBAL IDENTITY: THE CALENDAR OF THE FUTURE

In the past, methods of communication and means of transportation set limits upon the interaction of different cultural groups, but today those limits no longer exist. Using satellite transmission, telephone

and fax, communication is instantaneous, and with modern air transport, traveling time is measured in mere hours and minutes, not weeks and days.

Today the challenge is no longer how to measure and organize time or how to communicate that knowledge. Priests, scholars and scientists have already proven the calendar to be an extremely useful religious and social tool. Rather than providing for our spiritual well-being, the challenge now is to establish a calendar for use in a worldwide global community.

As our need for shared intercultural transactions, travel and communications grows, so does the need for a simple, accurate and universal calendar system. It may be necessary for the United Nations, or other appropriate international body, to take the lead. Through consultation with all interested governments, institutions and other groups, an international calendar and timekeeping system could be devised, that would spare international relationships the confusion of the current timekeeping Tower of Babel. On the other hand, the rich variety of the earth's many different cultural, national and religious groups would be able to continue joyously celebrating their distinctiveness, rejoicing at the time and in the way they wish.

The search for a unique identity, either religious, cultural or political, as expressed through special calendars, would give way to the search for a new international identity reflecting and confirming that the world and its people are an interdependent global community.

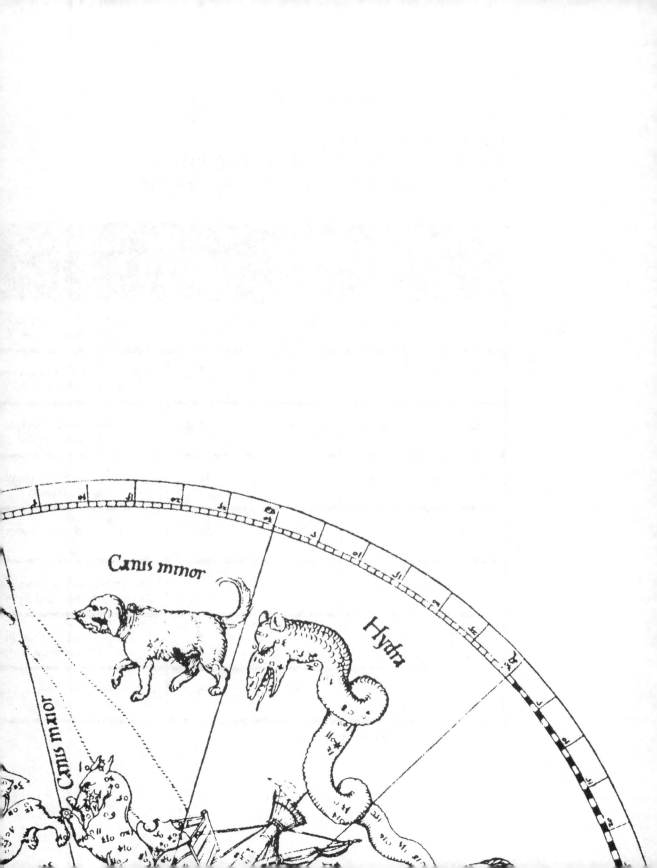

Canis minor

Canis maior

Hydra

APPENDIX

A SUMMARY OF IMPORTANT
CHARACTERISTICS OF EIGHT SELECTED CALENDARS.
(Dates in parentheses correspond to the Gregorian calendar.)

CALENDAR	TYPE	DAYS IN REGULAR YEARS	DAYS IN LEAP YEARS	INTERCALATION
HEBREW	Lunisolar	353, 354, or 355	383, 384, or 385	1 month added 7 times in each 19-year cycle
MAYAN	Solar	365	366	5 days added in common year 6 days in leap years
CHINESE	Lunisolar	353, 354, or 355	383, 384, or 385	1 month added 7 times in each 19-year cycle
ZOROASTRIAN	Lunisolar	365	395	5 days/year plus 1 month every 120 years
JULIAN	Solar	365	366	1 day added every 4 years
GREGORIAN	Solar	365	366	1 day added every 4 years, ex 3 of every 4 years ending in
HIJRI	Lunar	354	355	1 day added 11 times in each 30-year cycle
BADÍ'	Solar	365	366	4 days added in common year 5 days in leap years

* Months are given numbers, not names

MONTHS IN YEAR	DAYS IN MONTH	DIVISIONS SMALLER THAN A MONTH	BEGINS DAY AT:	MONTH IN WHICH YEAR BEGINS	TIME RECKONED FROM:
12 or 13	29 or 30	7-day week	sunset	Tishri (Aug–Sept)	Creation (3761 BC)
18	20	13-day unit	unknown	Pop (unknown)	unknown (3300 BC)
12 or 13	29 or 30	5-day & 10-day units	sunrise	No. 1* (20 Jan–19 Feb)	unknown (2397 BC)
12	30	none	sunrise	Fravartin (25 March)	exact date unknown
12	29 to 31	7-day week	midnight	January	Birth of Christ (AD 1)
12	28 to 31	7-day week	midnight	January	Birth of Christ (AD 1)
12	29 or 30	7-day week	sunset	Muharram (changes each yr.)	Hegira (AD 622)
19	19	7-day week	sunset	Bahá (21 March)	Declaration of the Báb (AD 1844)

BIBLIOGRAPHY

GENERAL

Adler, Irving and Ruth Adler. *The Calendar*. New York: John Day, 1967.

Bell, Thelma and Corydon Bell. *The Riddle of Time*. New York: Viking Press, 1963.

Boorstin, Daniel J. *The Discovers*. New York: Random House, 1983.

Coleman, Lesley. *A Book of Time*. New York: The Nelson Co., 1971.

Cowan, Harrison J. *Time and Its Measurement – From the Stone Age to the Nuclear Age*. New York: The World Publishing Co., 1958.

Hastings, James, editor. *The Encyclopaedia of Religion and Ethics*. New York: Charles Scribner's Sons, 1951.

Irwin, Keith G. *The 365 Days*. New York: Thomas Y. Crowell Co., 1963.

The Multifaith Calendar. Port Moody, Canadian Ecumenical Action, B.C., Canada. 1987.

The New Encyclopaedia Britannica. Chicago: 15th Edition, 1984 Macropaedia Volume 3.

Parise, Frank, editor. *The Book of Calendars*. New York: Facts on File Inc., 1982.

Smithsonian Institution. "The Maya Calendar." Washington, D.C.: Office of Public Information, The Department of Anthropology, 1987.

UNICEF, Wall Calendars for 1973 to 1987.

The World Almanac and Book of Facts. New York: Newspaper Enterprise Association, 1979 and 1984.

The World Book Encyclopedia. Volume 3. Chicago: World Book, Inc., 1988.

BADI' CALENDAR

Esslemont, J.E. "Bahá'í Calendar, Festivals and Dates of Historic Significance." *The Bahá'í World, Vol. XVII*. Haifa: Bahá'í World Centre, 1981.

Forghani, Baher. *Days to Remember – A Compilation*. Mona Vale, N.S.W.: Bahá'í Publications Australia, 1983.

Holley, Horace. *Religion for Mankind*. London: George Ronald, 1956.

GREGORIAN CALENDAR DEVELOPMENT

Blair, Peter Hunter. *An Introduction to Anglo-Saxon England*. London: Cambridge University Press, 1962.

Crawford, S.J. *Byrhtferth's Manual (AD 1011)*. London: Early English Text Society, Oxford University Press, 1929. Available in Reprint.

Harrison, Kenneth. *The Framework of Anglo-Saxon History to AD 900*. Cambridge: University Press, 1976.

Michels, Agnes Kirsopp. *The Calendar of the Roman Republic*. Princeton, N.J.: Princeton University Press, 1967.

Partington, S.W. *The Danes in Lancashire*. Manchester, England: E.J. Morten Publishers, first published 1909, reprinted 1973.

Stenton, F.M. *Anglo-Saxon England*. Oxford: Clarendon Press, 1977.

HEBREW CALENDAR

Burnaby, The Rev. Sherrard Beaumont. *Elements of The Jewish and Muhammadan Calendars*. London: George Bell and Sons, 1976.

Encyclopaedia Judaica, Volume 5. Jerusalem: Keter Publishing House Ltd., 1971.

Penner, Lester. *The Jewish Calendar*. New York: L. Penner, n.d.

Shulman, Albert M. *Gateway to Judaism*, Volume 1. Cranbury, N.J.: Thoma Yoseloff, 1971.

Werblowsky, R.J. Zwi and Geoffrey Wigoder, editors. *The Encyclopedia of Jewish Religion*. New York: Holt, Rinehart, and Winston Inc., 1965.

Zerubavel, Eviatar. *The Seven Day Circle – The History and Meaning of the Week*. New York: The Free Press, 1985.

HINDU CALENDAR

Basham, A.L. *The Wonder That Was India*. New York: Taplinger Pub. Co., 1968, third edition.

Ross, Nancy Wilson. *Three Ways of Asian Wisdom*. New York: Simon and Schuster, 1966.

HIJRI CALENDAR

Abdalati, Hammudah. *Islam In Focus.* Indianapolis: American Trust Publications, 1975.

Lunde, Paul. "Science: The Islamic Legacy." *Aramco World Magazine* reprint for EXPO 86. Washington, D.C.: Aramco Corp., 1986.

— "The Turn of a Century". *Aramco World Magazine.* July–August 1979, Washington, D.C.: Aramco Corp., 1979.

Nawwab, Ismail I., Peter C. Speers and Paul F. Hoye, editors. *Aramco And Its World – Arabia And The Middle East.* Washington, D.C.: Aramco Corp., 1980.

UNWRITTEN TIMEKEEPING

Burl, Aubrey. *Prehistoric Stone Circles.* Aylesbury, Bucks, U.K.: Shire Publications Ltd., n.d.

Chippindale, Christopher. *Stonehenge Complete.* London: Thames and Hudson, 1983.

Duran, Diego. *Book of the Gods and Rites of the Ancient Calendar.* Translated and edited by Fernando Horcasitas and Doris Hayden. Norman: University of Oklahoma Press, 1971.

Hawkins, Gerald S. *Stonehenge Decoded.* Garden City, N.J.: Double Day and Co. Inc., 1965.

Hiatt, L.R., editor. *Australian Aboriginal Concepts.* Canberra: Australian Institute of Aboriginal Studies, 1978.

Krupp, E.C. *Echoes of the Ancient Skies – the Astronomy of Lost Civilizations.* New York: Harper & Row Pub. Inc., 1983.

Massola, Aldo. *The Aborigines of South-eastern Australia – As They Were.* Melbourne: William Heinemann Australia Pty Ltd., 1971.

National Geographic Book Service. *The World of the American Indian.* Washington, D.C.: National Geographic Society, 1989.

Renfrew, Colin. *Before Civilization.* New York: Alfred A. Knopf, 1973.

Williamson, Ray A. *Living the Sky – The Cosmos of the American Indian.* Line illustrations by Snowden Hughes. Boston: Houghton Mifflin Co., 1984.

RECOMMENDED FOR YOUNG READERS

Brindze, Ruth. *The Story of Our Calendar.* New York: Vanguard Press Inc., 1949.

Gaer, Joseph. *Holidays Around The World.* Boston: Little, Brown and Co., 1953.